How To
Like Everything:

A Utopia

How To
Like Everything:

A Utopia

Paul Shepheard

Winchester, UK
Washington, USA

First published by Zero Books, 2013
Zero Books is an imprint of John Hunt Publishing Ltd., Laurel House, Station Approach,
Alresford, Hants, SO24 9JH, UK
office1@jhpbooks.net
www.johnhuntpublishing.com
www.zero-books.net

For distributor details and how to order please visit the 'Ordering' section on our website.

Text copyright: Paul Shepheard 2012

ISBN: 978 1 78099 820 6

A CIP catalogue record for this book is available from the British Library.

Design: Stuart Davies

Printed and bound by CPI Group (UK) Ltd, Croydon, CR0 4YY

We operate a distinctive and ethical publishing philosophy in all
areas of our business, from our global network of authors to
production and worldwide distribution.

CONTENTS

How To Like Everything is a utopia.

'Utopia' is a word invented five hundred years ago at the start of the modern age as a description of the ideal society. It's composed of Latin parts that taken together mean 'no place' or 'nowhere'. We now use the word utopia to mean an impossible dream of perfection. How To Like Everything recasts the actual world, the forever changing world we already live in, as utopia – to make the impossible possible.

1
Everything

"I am going back again, and will seek to refresh myself with the things that I then cast away for hopes of which I now see is not."
John Bunyan, *The Pilgrim's Progress:* the atheist

1

The Atheist's Progress

This is a book about everything. It's a big subject, so I'm going to start with a story and then I'm going to ask a question.

Here's the story:

Once upon a time there was a girl, called Little Red Cape, who was wandering in a forest. The forest was full of confusions. Some were ugly and some were delightful, but they existed in such plenty that it was possible to spend every minute of your life amongst them without noticing you were getting any older. Little Red Cape knew she was lost, but she didn't care. She was supposed to be carrying a basket of eggs to her grandmother's house. She had been told that the way to get through the confusion of the forest was to follow the paths that had been built between the houses, like strings in a maze, to keep from getting lost; and she'd started off down the path, but she soon found it so overgrown with the forest's confusions that she had become interested in them, and she'd dilly dallied, and that's how she'd gone astray.

You know this story. Little Red Cape is Little Red Riding Hood, or, as they say in Holland, Rood Kapje. The original is a Grimm Brothers' tale of warning, about the terrors of the wide world. The second part of my story is not so familiar:

There were other creatures in the forest that had different ways of living amidst all the confusion. They maintained a tight hierarchy between the members of their packs and they elaborated their lives in rituals, as when they gathered together in circles to howl at the moon. And recently they had discovered that the humans were losing the keys to the locks that kept their houses safe, and discovered that if they wanted to they could simply walk in and eat the humans

up and live there themselves. Maybe they were impressed by the
power that the houses manifested. Maybe they thought that by
inhabiting them, they could share the humans' power. But the fact
was that the howling and the hierarchies were incorporated into
domestic life; and so you could say that with this development the
forest became even more confusing than ever.

So that's the story – it's an analogy for today's world. Who the
wolves are and who the humans are I am not yet sure; but little
Red Cape is you. The forest in the story is not a labyrinth or a
metaphor for the workings of your inner mind, it is a picture of
a complex field. A picture of the actual world.

And here's the question. What will you do, Little Red Cape?
Will you go on searching for your grandmother's house, with all
the risks that that entails? Or will you remain out among the
confusions – with all the risks that *that* entails?

A LITTLE WHILE AGO I suddenly had this thought: I have to
get my ideas on television. I wanted to stalk the world in sharp
clothes speaking to camera like all those other guys. But I soon
found out that this attack of ego, this yearning for the varnish of
fame, was as doomed as a night on the Big Brother tiles. I
discovered that my thoughts were far too chaotic for the
medium. I had hundreds of bits and pieces flying about in my
head, which spewed out into my trial scripts like one damned
cornucopia after another.

"Look, Paul," said the film maker I was working with. "Keep
it simple." He was exasperated by rewrite four, which had
turned out even more convoluted and baroque than rewrite
three. "Are you listening to me?" He said. "Keep it simple. In a
one-hour television programme you can say three things, okay?
First, you say what you're going to say. Second, you say it. And
third – you say what you just said."

Look at them! It's true! That's exactly what they do. They say something, say it again, and then say it a third time. So I sent the television script files to the recycle bin and changed my computer desktop background to a crazy mimetic-expressionist painting by Asger Jorn that looks like a food fight at a childrens' party, and started on what you have here. At the time I had been reading Tom Stoppard's play *The Coast of Utopia* in book form, speaking the parts to myself, imagining myself into all the characters and their clothes and their voices and exits and entrances, and as I was reading I thought that this is what all books are: they're scripts. Writers write scripts for their readers to perform. Like an actor performing a play, when you read a book you bring something to it that only you can. When you watch television, you sit back as sceptical as a child being lectured to, only half listening to what's said, passing notes to the others in the room and counting the hairs growing out of the teacher's nose. When you read a book you get involved, you *act*; you perform what you read in the theatre of your imagination, enriched and costumed and all lit up with your own knowledge and your own memories and your entire history.

The title of this project, *How to Like Everything*, started out with a smaller ambition: *How to Like Art*. That was the pitch of the first draft of the first TV script. It all began because I wanted to pin down the confusion of contemporary art. I wanted to say that today's art is so full of the revelations of philosophy and science that it has become criticism, and no longer art: and so full of discrimination and fury, as a consequence, that artists have to hitch their wagons to an explanation of what they do before they've even done anything. The explanation has become the artwork. The thing itself is a mere illustration of its own story: notoriously, the shark, the bed, the pile of bricks. This is not news to you, everyone knows it. But the question I wanted to ask was not how to know whether something was good art, not even whether it was worth the asking price - but what is art itself? Maybe even – *What bloody use is it?*

Now, after looking at it and talking about it, and reading French philosophy *till the cows come home*, and *biting my nails* and *grinding my teeth* and *tossing and turning* and *having nightmares* about it, even getting into a fist fight about it on one terrible occasion, my project has ballooned into *How To Like Everything*. Because now I understand that art, philosophy and science are parts of a piece – they work together. Art, Philosophy and Science are the enquiry engines of culture, our attempts to work out what the world means to us. Because the world is continuously unfolding, it needs continual reinterpretation. And the same confusions that shiver the world of art are also present in philosophy and science, threaded through all three of them like doubt is threaded through faith. For the last hundred years Science has set the pace by throwing into view the invisible forces: quantum physics, relativity, genetics and evolution. These four are the contemporary frames for understanding our world and they are all sub-perceptual. They can't be seen or touched. I call them *dark knowledge*. It means that the world we experience and the world we know about are different. It's as though the material world has taken on a metaphysical aspect. Perhaps it has always been this way. This dark knowledge we all live with occupies the territory that religion used to occupy, when philosophy, not science, is what came first.

So I'm setting out to write a sort of pilgrim's progress, a journey through this invisible new wilderness, through the confusions arising from the clash between that re-engineered metaphysics and the mundane world. Things have been this way before: *The Pilgrim's Progress* is an enduring nonconformist tract of the seventeenth century by John Bunyan, and in that, the pilgrim, named Christian, treads his path through confusion determined to find the gates of heaven and escape it altogether. Like everyone else, I used to think that a critic's job is to clear up confusion. But now I don't want to escape it, I want to touch it, understand it, *like* it; so this book's journey is to be *The Atheist's*

Progress. There is an atheist in Bunyan's work. He appears very briefly. He comes and goes in twenty lines. He encounters Christian near the end of his search at the top of a mountain and laughs out loud when he hears what the man is up to. He says that Christian is wasting his time looking for the gates of heaven and then he disappears from the book, cheerfully striding back down the mountain to immerse himself again in the complexity of the world. While the Pilgrim plods his straight and narrow way searching for clarity, the Atheist, chortling to himself, plunges back into the temptations and the confusions of life because that's where living creatures belong.

What a great guy! Quite unlike today's celebrity atheists. They don't laugh at all – they are flat out angry. They rant and rage against creationists who want to teach the book of Genesis in school science. "Evolution is a scientifically proven fact!" They howl. They want to destroy everything but the truth. My atheist – Bunyan's atheist? – is not out to destroy anything. He thinks that science is a matrix of knowledge, not of truth; that *Utopia* could be found in the reconciliation of the creation story with the theory of evolution; and surely, he suggests – if we teach the children everything we think as well as everything we know, they can learn to think for themselves?

The laughing atheist. He does not reason his lack of faith, but feels it. It is a matter of emotion, not reason. He believes his lack of faith. He believes in nothing, lucky man: and so finds the freedom to start to like everything.

2

The World Whisperer

I am writing this in Amsterdam, Holland, the Netherlands, in an old Amsterdam canal-side house so lofty and with stairs so steep it has a crane on the top to hoist furniture up from the street and in through the huge windows. My studio overlooks the Old Church. The Dutch call it *De Oude Kerk*. One of Amsterdam's ancient canals flows past the front door, its surface dark green and full of reflections. The water inches by as slowly as the hands of the church clock. Yesterday a discarded television took all morning to float past, looking like a commentary on the futility of contemporary life, if your mind is of the sort that will wander that way. The canal moves in response to Amsterdam's complicated regime of water management, which keeps the sea outside the dikes at bay. We are living below sea level here. Global warming is not some future terror for the Dutch; the movement of the tides and the level of the sea is their continuous present. The story so far is that the Old Church has been standing over there on the other side of the canal for maybe six hundred years. It fills my window with its ancient asymmetries and wonderful colours, a picture so solid and true it pushes out doubt. And yet, where we are is also what they call the Red Light District. All around me the little streets and alleys are filled with whores. They stand at the windows in their bras and pants pouting and knocking on the glass at the tourists who throng here night and day – and at me whenever I leave the house – and at the seagulls that flock the canals, come to that. They do it at everything. In the afternoons the sun hits the west front of the church like a clapper striking a bell and the pimps stand on the corners like policemen on duty and the seagulls screech round and round looking for something to steal and the whores stand and perform their sexual mimes. The picturesque and the salacious are all mixed together in this place like an emulsion.

Which is good, I think, because I am here, in this tall, canal-side house paid for by the art school, trying to make sense of my proposition *How To Like Everything;* this idea that crawled out of my head maybe two years ago now and has been lying at my feet writhing like a pole dancer ever since while I try to integrate it. And maybe that word 'emulsion' is what I want. An emulsion is a fluid where everything is not dissolved in the water but ubiqui-tously mixed – the particles are held together in suspension. Maybe that's what needs to be done. Can I call myself an emulsionist? Keep all the balls in the air at once? Something so enticing and so complicated as *How To Like Everything* might not integrate, might not solve – might not *dissolve* – after all.

"Why do you want to do this?" My Dutch friends say. They whom my wife Lola calls *the Inquisition.* They travel in a pack of three and ask questions non-stop. Except when they giggle. They giggle like naughty boys. "What use is it to like everything?" they giggle. "Do you like torture? Do you like bombs? It's so hard to like everything!" Collapsing in giggles. Once I visited some American friends, she the architect, he the painter of large grey canvases of girls on the edges of nervous breakdowns. He had a huge vinyl collection, as young men all did at that moment in history, but unusually it was a widely eclectic mix of stuff – he played Ella Fitzgerald, then Bartok, then Kate Bush, then The Chemical Brothers, then Coltrane – it was lovely.

"Oh sure, I like every kind of music, music is like the ocean. It swirls around the globe and connects us all up," he said. I couldn't have agreed more. It was lovely! I once drove for three hours across the desolate Rannoch Moor, highlands, Scotland, UK, with my silent fifteen year old son, my eldest son now grown up and left home, listening to the heavy metal band Metallica – his choice – and I have loved that record ever since. And now it was so warm and giving in the broad ambience of this painter's music collection, this man who liked every kind of music, that I wanted to hear it again – can we hear some Metallica? I said.

"Hell no, man, I don't listen to that shit."

"But, but, but..." I stuttered, completely stalled by this about face. I searched lamely, mistakenly, for some description of the band's quality to justify my choice: "but they're so *precise!*"

"And that's all they are," he scowled.

It's not enough to believe in nothing. To like something you have to frame its qualities somehow – which is why, when cornered, I called Metallica 'precise' – but then I could have said 'mathematical'. I could have said 'sweaty'. A quality is only a part of the story, part of the explanation; something your mind can grab hold of. There we were arguing over Metallica, when in actuality there was no Metallica present, only a chimera of Metallica in our heads. Things – and do all atheists think that people are things, or is it just me? – things exist in the world in all their actual complexity, but a thing is only itself, not an idea but a thing: one of countless millions of things in the world. Why do we try to overcome this? Why are we so keen to simplify and rank and grade? Is it innate or is it something we laboriously learn from infanthood on?

THE DOORBELL RINGS. A Jehovah's Witness is standing there on the doorstep in her perky mauve hat and her old fashioned suit, holding a little briefcase. She is working the red light district. A lone snowplough out after a heavy fall. She takes out a picture of planet earth taken from space and shows it to me; the blue green brown globe hanging in the blackness, swirled with clouds, incandescent with the reflected light of the sun – it's beautiful and complex – it's a picture of everything! Is my first thought. Everything on Earth is too small to see in that photo, but it's all there.

Her opening question is: how can you believe something so complex and beautiful as this was not made by a greater power?

In the beginning there was chaos, and then God made the world, is her story, and – she goes on – "now look, it's full of confusion because we've lost our way." She says do I have any thoughts on that? And I think this: in the beginning, the world was perfect and then god came along and changed it into something else. Or was it the devil? Can you believe in the devil and not believe in god?

"Look," I say, "You may get me to agree that god exists. Something's got to explain the grief and the strife. But you'll never convince me that he created the world." And it takes me an hour and a half to persuade her that I mean it, standing there on the doorstep while the traffic of the sinful world passed by.

And now I am swept by anxieties and doubts. I switch on the coffee machine and wait while it does its little gulps and snorts. I try to get my thoughts straight. Daylight pours through the studio window kissing every surface just as it has for two hundred years, but the grace of god it used to kiss with has turned, during that time, into a cascade of photons. The drips of coffee scud across the surface in the jug like atoms in an experiment. The percolator growls. Tiny bursts of steam escape as the water turns from liquid to gas – but has science taught us anything? Every day, we watch the sun coming up in the east and going down in the west even while knowing that what we see is the Earth going round the sun. Everyday we are at each other's throats, locked in ancient enmities, even while knowing we are one humanity. How could life illuminated by science still be so confusing? Is it that the everyday fact of hurtling through space, hugged by the coincidence of a water-laden atmosphere, spinning towards a future when the sun itself will eventually explode, is too terrible to look at?

I stamp round the studio, my head running hot, babbling that our fear of dark knowledge is what god fearing has become. And all around us people attempt to overcome it by grasping at this and that firm thing, history, sustainability, ethnicity, gender; they strap on a bit tighter the blinkers of holy books; they gorge on sword and sorcery stories; and at the same time as they're doing all that, they go and decode the genome and try to recreate the Higgs boson.

Suddenly, the Inquisition is here again. They burst through the door in the middle of my rant and clattered up the steep stairs and started to raid the liquor cupboard before they even sat down.

"I don't know much about art, but I know what I like," says one.

"I know a lot about art and I like a lot of it," says the next.

"I know everything about art and I like everything," says the last, and they collapse into giggles all over the floor. I stay as silent as a stoic.

They keep at it: "Why do you want to do this? What use is it to like everything? Do you like torture? Do you like bombs?"

They want Margaritas. Six shots of Tequila, distilled from cactus juice, three of Curacao liqueur with its bitter whiff of Caribbean oranges, and the juice of two limes. Plenty of ice, then a little more ice. Shake it up and pour it out.

Why do I want to like everything? I survey their beaming faces. Lit up with mock expectation and brimming with giggles. Ready to send their cocktails spluttering back into the glasses through their nostrils. And okay, I say to them holding up my hands like a burglar at bay: it is a peculiar idea. When the first seven years of our lives are spent learning to sort the wrong from the right and the good from the bad, and the rest of our time on earth actively sorting them. And when everything we do is based on discrimination and judgement, on making decisions and getting them right; when all our hopes are for a better world, when all our striving is for excellence and we value goodness as highly as breathing – *speak for yourself*, says the pimp on the corner, *what I do is make a better world for me. The girls come in on trains from the East and I shmooze them into coming with me because*

believe me man I can be charming when I want to be, then I lock them
up in a darkened room and hit them with wooden planks until they're
softened up and I can put them to work.

Maybe that's it. Maybe the pimp is doing what we all do. We whack the world with planks until it softens up enough for us to change it. Why do we want to change it? Maybe we still believe the old story, in which we were cast out of paradise. Where when you're hungry all you have to do is open your mouth and the food jumps into it. Where the ground has no hills to climb and you want for nothing. And we were cast out of that into this terrifying, hostile place, full of ice and mountains and toil: the wilderness. And we set-to whacking it back into shape. Whacking it soft, whacking it smooth. Getting it back to paradise. And we're still doing it.

"You pussy!" say the Dutchmen. "Who do you think you are – the world whisperer?!"

They mean like *horse whisperer*. They are teasing me but I like the sound of it, *The World Whisperer*. And I tell them that if people liked everything, they wouldn't behave like that towards the world, or towards each other. The torture and the bombs could be put back on the shelf.

"So what about disease?" They yell. "How do you like that?" And then – suddenly swerving off on a tangent – "How did Aids get started?" They stare at each other, bursting with giggles. "It was a monkey plague for years then all of a sudden it's in the humans. How did that happen?" They are pretending to want someone to blame. Pretending not to see Aids as emergent nature, but as an invasion.

"Come on put your hand up!" they yell, as immoderately as the gutter press, laughing and pushing each other like school kids. "Who was it?! Who was it who fucked the monkey?" We laugh and laugh and laugh.

And then fall to quarrelling about the provenance of that joke. I tell them I've heard it at least twice before, and so the discussion transmutes: of what value is originality? Is it, like beauty and authenticity, triggered by emotion? The materialist in me says that everything is emotional, everything is authentic, beautiful and original. Every particle is a one-off. Every joke is new-every-morning. But whether that rates originality as high value or low value or the only value we cannot agree.

BACK IN ENGLAND, in the Cedars Care Home, my aged mother is sitting in a special old person's chair with a big spring in it and a lever at the side that can raise her up to standing position. She's five hundred kilometres away but I know she is sitting there because that's what she does all day long, day after day. She spends her time amongst forty other oldsters with a combined age of three and a half thousand. Collectively they are as old as Stonehenge. They sit there in a circle for long hours without uttering a sound, like menhirs on the plain. I call the care home *Spaceship Cedars*. If I walk in there with my little boy Jackie, strange customer that he is, everyone is riveted. In spite of everything, he carries the magic branch of youth, and they love him for it. You can see it in their eyes when they look at him; yes! There is hope!

Everything is emotional because hope is. It took the sight of this happy bunch of shipwrecks in the Cedars Care Home to make me see it and now I can't stop. When I talk to people I no longer see rational beings engaged in rational discourse, I see objects, emoting. It has made me such a deep materialist that I see everything as objects, people, dogs, trees, rocks – objects that burn with the animation of hope, each engaged in their own private miracle of being. And the things that people make, the buildings and machines, the paintings and the poems, are artificial miracles, which glow with light borrowed from their makers.

"Hey, World Whisperer," comes a shout. And the three of them are grinning and jiggling their empty glasses at me like a bunch of monkeys.

3

Family Life

THE ROAD OUTSIDE is just beginning to heave with the restless commerce of the night, and the house is all lit up, tall as a tower. The boy in his rocket ship pyjamas climbs the steep stairs in front of me, his little head ascending into the volume above. With one hand he is holding onto both the banister rail and a large plastic robot, with the other an open comic, and clenched under his armpit is a huge dark-blue hard-back dictionary, embossed in gold. Progress is slow. He goes up the stairs one at a time, leading with his left foot and waiting till his right foot joins it on the tread before moving on to the next. It's a shuffle. He knows how to climb stairs like the rest of us, but he never remembers to.

"Come on Trogo, leg over leg," I prompt him, putting my hand in the middle of his back and giving a tiny shove. Jackie is his name, *Trogo* is his nickname. He gets his legs working properly and we speed up but at the same time he leans back against my hand harder and harder as he goes until I am supporting most of his forty kilos on one hand and getting concerned about my own stability. Suddenly reaching the top of the stairs becomes an issue, suddenly I see how dangerous it is, suddenly I realise we might break both our necks in a backwards fall, and there we are, suddenly – another everyday event rushed to the edge of panic.

"Jackie! Stand straight! Not on the stairs!" I yell at him, and he stops and turns round and his beautiful open face is laughing as he leans forward and tips himself over and falls upon me, forcing me to grab for the banister. The robot springs from his hand and bumps back down the stairs, breaking apart and spinning plastic pieces everywhere, and the big dictionary slips from his arm and falls, pages fluttering, to crack open its spine when it hits the floor. Adrenalin floods me and I heave him up, heavy as a sack of stones, onto the half landing. My heart is thudding like a hammer. Jackie giggles all over, delighted with the catastrophe and still as unsteady as a wobbly toy, teetering on the brink of falling off the landing and crashing down the stairs himself. I can feel the fury starting, tickling the roots of my hair – but I started this. And it wasn't even that I wanted him to go up the stairs faster; I wanted him to go up like other little boys do. I am a bigger fool than he is. So I move into gruff wolf mode, bushing my eyebrows and snarling and tickling him in the ribs to bring him back to reality, snapping the light switch on in mock anger and growling out his favourite phrase, "Pent up rage! Pent up rage!," already ninety five percent drawn into his silly game myself.

Ninety-five percent? That's the quantity of genes that humans, *Homo sapiens*, share with chimpanzees. And what an astonishing reality it is, that we are so close to the apes. The chimpanzees' Latin name is *Pan troglodytes* – hence Jackie's nickname. When he first appeared in the world after forty-eight hours hard labour and an emergency caesarean his features were so squashed up I thought he looked like a chimp: *Trogo*, I called him. But ninety-five percent? That's a lot. Why not call humans *Pan sapiens*? The 'chimps that are wise'?

I remember visiting the anthropological museum in London to see the exhibit on the early hominids. *Homo habilis* – the 'toolmaker' – *Homo erectus* – who 'walked upright'. *Homo neanderthalensis*, the Neanderthals. But the earliest hominid known at that time was not *Homo* anything, but *Australopithecus afarensis* – the petrified skeleton of a girl, three and a half million years old, found in what is now Afar, in Ethiopia. The museum had a plaster model of her, standing in a glass case like a mannequin in a shop window. Except that she was only one metre tall. She had straggly black hair and wood brown skin and tiny little breasts. She was so cute! She was standing there among the rocks and litter of the Tanzanian rift valley, in front of a painted backdrop of African skies, looking as though she was facing her future, and the future of humankind. And what I knew that Jackie was going to have to go through in his own future suddenly overwhelmed my heart. The tears welled up and the other people looked at me brimming over like a baby; and then – another surprise – humanism, with all its succour and all its hindrance, slowly slid off me and finally left me alone. And welcomed me to the planet of the apes.

So now, fuss over, bum wiped, hands washed and teeth brushed, this scatty little ape is climbing into his huge bed. He has this bed in case he has a bad night and needs one of us with him. He always used to have trouble in his cot; he never learned how to do it. He used to fling his arms out and get them stuck in the bars and we'd come rushing in to attend to his cries and find him pinioned flat on his back in the shape of a cross like some ghoulish Flemish painting of the baby Jesus with the future already configured. So we would all end up in one bed sleeping in a tangle of limbs and eventually, when he was too big for it and no one was getting any sleep, we realised what we needed was two double beds between the three of us.

"Come on dad, get in," he says.

"What me? In there? In my jeans and everything?" Feigning shock as usual.

"Come on dad."

So in I get in my jeans and everything and I pull the covers over us and I put my arm round him and he puts his little head on my chest and grins at me. That grin means *this is paradise* and he's right, it is. There is no better place to be than in bed with one you love. I close my eyes and pretend to go to sleep.

"Story." He says. *Storwee.* I give out a great pretend snore. He clamps his teeth on my shirt collar and digs his finger into my neck and says it again. *Schstoorweee!*

Are we comfortable? Pillows okay? Duvet under chin? Then

I'll begin.

Once upon a time there was a little girl.

"I mean ugly duckling," says Jackie. By which *he* means 'you mean'. So who gets pronouns these days? We could do away with them altogether. We could call everyone and everything 'it'. "It means ugly duckling." But this is a different story, Jacko: I'll start again.

Once upon a time there was a little girl lost in a forest. It was beautiful, this place, not frightening, and the beauty of it is what had got her lost. She was looking for her grandmother's house, looking everywhere, under rocks, behind trees, among the leaves and flowers, when suddenly she came face to face with a wolf! And what a face it was! Huge mouth, huge teeth, "Huge eyes!" Jackie says.

The wolf opened up his huge mouth and swallowed the little girl right up, just like that.

Jackie's head is in the sleeping position on my chest but his eyes are still wide open. What is he thinking, my enigmatic boy? To whom conversation is almost as hard as it is to a chimpanzee? Shelves full of robots line the walls of his room like a plastic terracotta army; maybe he's thinking they can be pressed into service to help Little Red Cape out.

So when Little Red Cape arrived in the stomach of the wolf she found her grandmother in there, looking all slimy and pathetic, and the two of them were crammed together in the wolf's belly and the wolf ran all the way to her grandmother's house, which he had made his home. He opened the door and jumped on the bed and tried to go to sleep so he could digest them both but Little Red Cape pushed her hand right up his throat and forced his teeth apart with her fingers to make a speaking tube and yelled as loud as she could.

The philosophical implications of this story, the being and the understanding, the knowing, the acting – they've sent my boy to sleep. Little Trogo with his porcelain eyelids like an eighteenth century beauty. His aunt Sally reads bedtime stories in a dumb monotone, as slow and boring as she can, to send his cousins to sleep. I prefer to do it by philosophical overload. *And keep it simple, says the director.* Except that this is turning into a true story. And now I have to finish it for myself while my little one, my precious cargo, slumbers in peace, and I lie on my back still as a predator, so as not to wake him. I watch the ceiling all fretted with the rapidly moving shadows of urban life, and I listen to the sound of sirens and cat fights in the huge world outside.

Oh woodman! She yelled, oh man with the sharp knives, come and save us! Come and kill the wolf! She screamed. And when she had been freed, she went right on yelling. "Kill all the wolves!" She screamed. And that's just what the people did. They killed all the wolves. That's why the world is a better place than it was before.

JACKIE'S MOTHER LOLA came in on a midday flight to Schipol this afternoon, and he and I went to meet her off the plane. She is always travelling. She has a pile of air miles as big as the pyramids and her jet lag keeps her in an ethereal state of mind that she calls *Club Class*. "I can't think right now," she says, "I'm in Club Class." I like to imagine she works in anti-terror. She says she is in the clerking department but she is so glamorous to my eyes I think of her when she is away from home as James Bonding it through jungles with guns and kick boxing and swimming out to yachts in blue water in thousand dollar bikinis. She denies it, but I reason it out – if it were true she couldn't tell me, could she? Jackie and I could just be part of her cover story. I have to say she's very good at the concealment. She teases me sometimes and tells me I should get a job in global warming, and then we'd have the twin terrors of the modern world covered. When I told the Inquisition this, the Dutch guys with their flowery shirts and their long toed shoes: "Oh yes," they said, not smiling at all, "twin terrors, twin towers, very funny. But we all work in global warming, don't we? That's what work is."

Why stop there? Why stop at work? That's what *life* is – that's what breathing is! You can see it on a cold day, the carbon exhaust smoking out of people's lungs. Just being *alive* is warming up the planet. Just everything we do. When Jackie and I walked through the wonderland of Schipol airport – he shuffling along in his funny over-toed walk, but not prepared to hold my hand, he's like any other boy sometimes – the background noise, the noise of industry and commerce, filled the huge spaces with a hushed hum. The whole place seeps greenhouse gases like one huge flue. Schipol is not just an airport but a thriving hive of fifty thousand workers. Not just a transport hub but a town, with office buildings, warehouses, restaurants, shopping malls and parking lots. Outside there is the periodic rush of noise as the big airliners are hefted into the sky; but inside the terminal building what you have is this soft ambience of air conditioning and coin tinkling and credit card swiping, plus the drone of baggage wheels and the echo of announcements. The smell of the coffee.

We joined the other people waiting by the arrivals door, which powered open and closed as the travellers come out one by one, poor old Trogo getting beside himself with anxiety every time it was not his mum. He can't do future, Jackie. He only does present. If there's a describable future in his life – in this case, *she will soon come through that door* – he abandons everything but that. When he's waiting for supper back at home in the evenings he circles the kitchen like a dog. When he eats he can't wait to finish the plateful, he crams everything in in one huge unchewable mouthful, gasping for air. I sometimes think it's not a question of passing time, the way Jackie lives his life, but a question of space, as though he lives the big and the little at one and the same time. I hugged him and said, *Hey Jacko, don't sweat the everything stuff.* And when she at last came through the door, beaming like a spotlight, *Lola! We're over here!* The three of us joined together in the ecstatic present, and scooted off towards the train in a sweet space of gifts, kisses, smiles and laughter. It was great to have our secret agent back.

THIS BOOK OF HOW TO LIKE EVERYTHING is partly about believing in nothing, so you can like everything, hence the Atheist's progress. Partly about knowing what you know, so you can like the things other people tell you not to like. But it's mostly about living in the present. That is the key to the whole thing and that's why it has this little boy. If there's one thing Jackie's taught us it's the vitality of each incoming second. Children bring your own past into the present as you watch them taking on the world piece by piece, and they bring up your own fears of the future when you fear for theirs. You educate them the best you can – but how do you do that? Do you show them the whole forest or just the paths? Do you help them prepare their minds for the wilderness of the *actual* world, with all its currents and gusts, or do you help them coordinate the complex of society's conventions, that placeless thing we call the *real* world, with all the shadow boxing and posturing that it entails? I sit next to Jackie in front of children's television sometimes, murmuring a sort of corrective commentary on the tricks and fouls and manipulations unfolding before us on the screen. Sitting beside his tousled head as his bright eyes light on some new make-up doll, say, advertised against the background of a schoolgirl's sleep over, with them lying on the bed in pink spangled outfits speaking into cell phones, kicking their legs like sirens, strutting their eight year old stuff. Or perhaps some new breakfast cereal with comedy jungle animals. *Given archetypal life by Rudyard Kipling trying to match a child's imagination to the terrors of colonialism,* I actually hear myself saying to him: and now stereotyped by the House of Kellogg, capering round the cereal bowl; as milk sloshes in spilling zanily everywhere in a parody of critical theory, a sort of gingham underground of wackiness within boundaries.

"Let him get messy!" Said Trogo's consultant at our first meeting, way back when we had the first inkling that something was wrong. "Let him get his hands right in the paint. Do you play with him, rough and tumble? Hmm?" as he tried to discern whether the boy's problems were figments of our own anxieties. This was back in the MMR scare days when a rumour flew round that it was the vaccinations that were causing autism and the doctors and social workers suddenly lined up in a sort of phalanx of health care, armoured with plastic riot shields made of science, trying to explain to the raw recruits of the parent's army about the technicalities of immunisation. "What?" we yelled, waving pages printed from alternative medicine websites, "you make them sick on purpose? You give them diseases deliberately? Are you stark staring mad?" – although those question marks on their own don't get the stress quite right – "What?" We yelled. "Are you stark staring mad?!!!"

Having to cope with the difference of Jackie is a big part of why I try to formulate *How To Like Everything*. My plan is to learn to take the material, accumulated, pregnant world of the present on the chin and not to escape into the empty future, where all plans work out just the way you want them to.

I HEAVE MYSELF OUT OF JACKIE'S BED and cross over to the window to peep out of the curtain. The whores and their clients are going at it full tilt. Maybe messing about with sex is messing about with the present, too. Maybe it's just what life forms do. But then, as I stand there folded in the curtains, an idea appears out of the miasma of confusions and takes shape. The shape of this book.

They say that Mozart composed in his head on walks in the woods, returning home to write out all the orchestral parts just as he had heard them. As opposed to Beethoven, who had to hammer out every note one by one in the terrible smithy of his suffering. That's life in the Premier League. For me, somewhere in the back row of the third division, creation takes the middle path, a bit of both, a bit of strife, a bit of luck. And on this night the luck is neither Mozartite nor Beethovian, but Bachist. I stand there and watch as *How To Like Everything* forms itself. A utopia of the present moment. A suite of five pieces. The Amsterdam Suite. Five short essays about everything: the first of which, *Tabula Scripta*, about fundamentalism, is already in the bag. Then there's *Cliff Face Earth*, about the globalisation habit and *Angeland*, about how everything comes into existence. What else? *The Only Possible World*, about reason. And lastly *The Bowl Of The Horizon*, about the dynamics of experience. Jackie lets out a sleeping moan in the bed behind me. And I'm ready to go.

How do you like everything? Believe in nothing, know what you know, live in the present. And here's dusk incoming. Darkness falling. Lola is still lying upstairs in a deep sleep, dormant for now. Reunion sex after her trips away always does that to her. After the press of excitement and the skin-tight fires and the grease and the spit and finally the deep core eruptions she hardly says a word. She goes out like a volcano slipping back under the ocean.

Back downstairs, I flip on the television and find an American chat show beamed in by satellite. Adam Sandler is sitting there in the couch; shadow boxing with his celebrity, unable to contain his glee at being famous. Being very funny about it, lots of stories about his mum and dad, she apparently only ever able to see her little boy. "What film star?" She says to everyone. "This is my little boy." She was unhappy about the fact that he and his girlfriend – call her fiancée, okay? – lived together unmarried. Why? Because of the sex of course. "My mom, she's so old fashioned. I said okay, mom, look it's time to tell you, we're getting married! We're going to the Bahamas for the honeymoon, I tell her, expecting her to be like really, really pleased, but she frowns and says, well, sweetheart what's the point of a honeymoon if you've…if you've…if I've what, mom? I have to say to her – if you've already had sex! She says. Okay, I tell her. Look mom I'll tell you what. We haven't done anal yet. What if we save anal for the honeymoon?"

Tabula Scripta

Ssssh-schwitt! Phflonk – Dunk! And a cheer from the crowd as the head drops into the basket. The limp limbed torso, still spouting blood from its neck like a hose, is toppled off the slab and into a waiting cart already half full of slick red bodies. Another grey-faced victim is pushed forward up the steps and manhandled into position and the heavy blade is hauled to the top of the frame. Ssssh-schwitt! Phflonk – Dunk!

This is adult work. X-rated activity. Enforcing utopia is a business that children wouldn't understand. Unless the grown-ups at this scene, sophisticated only as far as hope and revenge will take them, think that they are enacting a fairy tale; the one in which a beauty lies sleeping, spellbound, in amongst a thicket of thorns. An overgrowth so verdant and complex, so effloresced, that to rescue her you must draw your sword and cut it all away, head by bloody head. The sleeping beauty in this case, in revolutionary Paris, being liberty: who eventually wakes up and sees what was done for her sake, and kisses the world.

But liberty is a piece of human imagination. There is no freedom in the material world, where everything depends on its relations with everything else. No equality or brotherhood either, except in the human imagination. Our histories are full of sleeping beauty clearances, sometimes not so bloody, but sometimes bloodier still. And imagination attends most of them. Cleansings, purges, new starts, the sweeping away of the old, the in with the new. What for? To make the world a better place?

Meanwhile the actual world, by which I mean not the splintered world of the human artifice but the whole of the planet Earth and its cargo of forms, runs a different mode to the optimistic clearing and rebuilding, the hopeful erasing of tablets, that we engage in. The Earth itself is changing all the time, spinning through space, cooling and heating, flowering here, rupturing there, but it changes like a moving shadow changes, without purpose. Its mentor is the sun, whose own progress is a continuous mighty burn on the way to a massive explosion, a broadcasting of energy that promulgates diversity wherever it can lodge. And how well it has lodged here on Earth! Every *so often we glimpse the huge, endwarfing totality of it all and fear engulfs us. That's when we get the bulldozers out. Human imagination, however powerful a thing, is not strong enough to face up to the complex pointlessness of the sun's broadcast. We would rather set about manufacturing a new hope; and to do that we are prepared to face down the horrors of our own making. The liberty of the torsos. The equality of bloodbuckets. The brotherhood of heads.*

Let me tell you a story about the time Jackie was first in hospital. He was only a couple of years old, tiny as an animal. He lay there in bed with eyes like wet stones. He had suffered a series of seizures and Lola and I were waiting at his bedside for the doctor's prognosis. We sat motionless like those gorillas in the cage in the zoo, uncomprehending, waiting to be released, for what seemed like – is, in the gorillas' case – years; when suddenly the curtain was drawn aside and a stranger's face appeared. He said he was the curate at the local church and that on Sunday the congregation would be saying a prayer for the boy. He wanted to know if there was anything else he could do? It was immense in the middle of our despair to suddenly feel this press of the community, one we hadn't even known was there. Later, when the crisis had passed, my wife went to visit the vicar to thank him and returned with the news that she was taking the boy to be baptized, and also, that she was getting baptized herself! And to qualify for that, she had to attend bible classes! It was such a sudden escalation of spiritual warfare that I had to hang on to her to stop myself falling over.

Her bible studies consisted of going in detail through the gospel of St. Luke. One evening she returned from class shaking her bible, aghast at the radicalism of this man Jesus, this tough love merchant from the other side of history. " 'He who is not with me is against me,' " she shouted. She opened it at chapter nine, where he is sending forth his disciples without food, without staves – without sticks to protect themselves – and without money, sending them as lambs among wolves – and here's her point, she yelled, as she flung the book across the room – without even letting them say goodbye to their families! He demands that they ditch everything to follow him. "One of them asks if he can bury his dead father before he goes." No, says Jesus. "He says 'no'!" She squealed. "He says 'let the dead bury their own dead'!" 'No man, having but his hand to the plough and looking back, is fit for the kingdom of god.' Cleansings, purges, new starts, the sweeping away of the old, the in with the new. Jesus was full of it. "What do you think?" she said. "He had a sign on his office desk, engraved 'Do It Now!'?"

Two measures of fundamentalism there – one, the revolutionary, whose impulse is to clear away the history of privilege and make a new, uncompromised future. The other, the prophet, who wants to clear away corruption and decadence to regain paradise; to regain a lost past. But what about the present? The always with us, quite unclearable present? Are we doomed to always feel this discontent with where we are, to live in a perpetual winter of cleansing dreams and disappointed ideas? What other way is there?

It's a peculiar place for an irreligious soul to look, but I found one in Ignatius Loyola's chapel in Rome. Loyola was the founder of the Jesuits, a spiritual army ranked against the clearances being made by Protestant reformers of the sixteenth century. Who went sweeping out the attics of faith and knocking the heads off statues of saints in what is now known as the reformation. And Loyola's army was the spearhead of the Catholic Church's fight back, the Counter Reformation. You can visit the private chapel in his apartments next to the Jesuit church of Il Gesu, a plain barrel vault painted in an elaborate optical illusion that looks like a bowl of spaghetti Bolognese. Until you stand at the spot marked out in the middle of the floor and the whole thing springs into your perception as an ornate, rectangular room carved with cherubs and volutes. The counter form itself was the baroque. Not the unclut-tered horizon of the protestant fundamentalists, but a twisting, curving, heavily freighted exuberance, not clear, not flat, hardly even explainable; and now, five hundred years later, a secular transformation of the baroque has become a figure for multiplicity promoters. Who see in its dissolutions, in its folds and complications, an analogue of the actual world that can complicate the illusionary abstraction of the clearances.

"That spot in the middle of the floor," says the guide, a fresh-faced young novice Jesuit priest all the way from Korea, "is the God's eye view, from which everything in the chaotic world can be seen for what it is." Never mind god, I think to myself. What about us? And you see how this works? You don't render the world explicable by clearing away obstacles and irrelevances but by carefully considering all that lies before you. Because everything is relevant. The tabula rasa of the fundamentalists is an erased tablet – but that is not what the world is. What it is is a tabula scripta – one with all the writing, the accumulated fund of all its forms, pulsing, present and intact. How do you make a better world? There is no better world.

2
Values

The sea values nothing because it misuses nothing. Man overvalues everything. And when he realises the cost is pegged to his valuation, complains that he is being ruined. Which of course he is.

WH Auden, *The Sea and The mirror:* Prospero, after heaving his magic books into the ocean

4

Ignorance and Experience

You had to get there early, to get a place in the queue. Up at six a.m. and on the bus by half past. You had to get to Anello and Davide's shop down in Covent Garden before seven on a Saturday morning to stand any chance of getting what you wanted. Which was a pair of black Cuban heeled elastic sided Baba boots like the ones the Beatles wore, the ones with the seam down the middle. This was at the end of nineteen sixty two, with *Love me do!* bouncing out of every loudspeaker in London, and Baba boots were in such demand from us boys that the entire week's consignment from the factory was sold out twenty minutes after the shop opened. The queue stretched all the way down the street. At nine thirty they started letting us into the shop three at a time and all you did was say your size and colour, "Nine, black" – no time to say hello or goodbye – and hand over your fifteen pounds, and you were off up the street with the brown paper bag under your arm and the whole day ahead of you, which now, because you had some Baba boots, felt like a whole new life.

"Get what you wanted?" said the moddy face who came out after me, as we walked up the street.

"Nine, black," I said.

"I got tan," he said, and I thought, that colour looks like dog shit. Why would you go and do a thing like that?

I am trying to explain to my friend Katrina my past as a teenage dandy on the streets of London back in the swinging sixties. They are not how to like everything stories, but just the opposite – discrimination stories. About those teenage days when we all thought everything had to be just so. Just *this*, and not *that*. A young man is sure of nothing. He is surrounded by complexity, and he thinks that by driving stakes into the ground he can anchor his thoughts. And has no choice but to start with the simple stakes: this is good. That is not good. Dialectic grips his heart. And why is it or is it not good? Well, because – and so the massive job of coming to grips with the muddle of it all begins.

Katrina and I are sitting in the café by the ferry berth on the North side of Amsterdam's big waterway, looking back at the city itself lit by the low winter sunshine, at the long birm of the central station and the colourful spangles of the new buildings and the swirly baroque of the old. It makes me want to sing, that view. Katrina tells a story about taking her four-year-old son Jacob to a farm, the sort of place they set out the pigs and the chickens and the sheep for visitors to see. She is sitting across the table in front of an aubergine Panini and a single espresso that half fills her tiny cup. To my eyes she is another magnificent sight to compare with the city skyline; with her green eyes and her big beaked nose and her crazy wild hair. She looks like Rasputin, except that she radiates health. She is the healthiest looking person I have ever seen. To see her is to want to merge with her.

She says she is a vegetarian now. No more meat for her.

"Why?" I ask. "For heaven's sake!" She describes how her little boy had asked her why they keep pigs on farms. "Pigs don't give milk," he said. Right she said. They don't give eggs or wool, either. "Right," he said. "So what are they for?" The conversation went on all the way home, and by the time they got back it turned out that the little boy was happy to go on eating bacon even now he knew where it came from, but Katrina wasn't. Her answers had not been good enough for herself. So now she was a vegetarian.

She looks at me with a so-what expression. Pushes her fingers through her mad hair. "So what did you do with the boots?" she says.

Okay, now I had the whole set. I had a pair of skin tight

pinstripes flared to twenty inches at the boot, I had the boots, I had a short grey Donegal-tweed jacket with three inch vents custom made by John Stephen on the north side of Carnaby Street where you had the fittings in the shop window before an audience of keen dressers out on the street who gave thumbs up and thumbs down, and I had a pin collared oxford cloth white shirt with a thin black leather tie. And of course I had hair. And it was in this outfit that I stood on the stage of the Studio 51 Club one night, clutching a microphone, fifteen years old, in front of a rhythm and blues audience wreathed in steam and smoke all yelling at me to blow my harp.

My Harp! That I didn't know how to play! I was standing there dressed like a dandy but unable to move my feet, with my intestines grimly churning inside me: why? Because harps – harmonicas – were hot news. Because no band could get a booking at the club without a harmonica player, and some friend of my sister had told the manager of this band that I had a harmonica and could stand in the corner of the stage in my nice clothes and fake it for long enough for the crowd to be diverted by the quality of the drumming. It was a stupid plan, but the band got the gig on the strength of it and here's what happened, as the beat was pounding and the crowd was beginning to jeer and I was showing no sign of faking anything: suddenly a bony figure I'd never seen before, in a brown trench coat and the first ever mullet haircut in the world, leapt on to the stage, flourished his own tiny harp, grabbed the microphone from me and began breathing the blues. The crowd roared its approval and the manager hustled me off the stage and pressed cab fare into my young hands and pushed me out onto the street, where I stood listening to the sound of Chicago issuing from the basement. And the cheers of the crowd. I was relieved, but I was humiliated. And Christ, it was a long ride home. I slunk to my room like a rat.

That man in the brown trench coat was none other than Rod Stewart! Yes – the very same. Rod The Mod Stewart once stood in for me on the harmonica down at Studio 51. But he and I have never spoken again since.

WHOSE IDEA WAS IT that your childhood is a trap? And that growing up is a process of working out how to spring the lock and escape? Innocence is not a state of grace; it's a state of captivity. Some people are born with keys, some people work hard at finding their keys and some people have keys thrust upon them. The teenage hump I've just described was when the door of my own trap flew open suddenly and all the noise and complexity of the world came bursting in and engulfed me. In my life now those days of innocence glimmer like the cliffs on a receding horizon seen from the deck of a ship. I wonder whether you ever lose sight of them altogether behind the curvature of time.

But innocence is not the opposite of experience. My philosopher friend Kathryn once startled me with the opinion that innocence is idealist rubbish. She calls herself a pragmatist. She says that the innocence of little children is a romantic confusion, another piece of creationism designed to break your heart. Little children know nothing, that's all, she said: "They're not innocent, they're *ignorant*." It was like being punched by the truth! They're ignorant because they have no experience. *In my life now those days of ignorance glimmer like the cliffs on a receding horizon seen from the deck of a ship.* And that's how I describe it to Katrina, who is standing there as usual with her brains blinking like hazard lights. She who pounces on clichés, such as life being like standing on the deck of a ship.

But we are at that moment in fact standing on the deck of a ship: one of the ferries that cross between the north and south banks of Amsterdam's river IJ. Looking east the horizon is all new architecture, where the old docks are becoming housing areas, all built up in slabs of colour like a sweetshop counter, and to the west you can make out the cranes and silos of the new docks, built for the big new monster ships. No moss grows on the feet of the Dutch. They are busy all the time, making the world new. The water of the IJ is sweet, they say, meaning fresh water, not salt water like the sea. In fact it is locked and dammed and is thus not a river but an inland lake; but it has the aspect of ocean to it with its expanse of wind whipped waves, its blueness and traffic of ships the size of buildings. Huge barges ply up and down to and from the Rhine and the interior of the European continent carrying the trade of the world. They travel so weighed down by cargo that their gunnels run below the water, but at the same time they are like floating suburban houses, these things. The family Toyotas sit up on the foredecks ready to be craned ashore as though they were parked outside the front gate. And up by the wheelhouses the bargees and their families cultivate little gardens, with white painted fences and swings for the children and flowerpots and easy chairs and little wooden windmills that spin in the breeze. It seems like a parody of Dutch life, all neat and tidied up like a sitting room, but at the same time daily grappling with the inundating profundity of sea level.

Sea level is a Dutch speciality. Huge chunks of the country lie below sea level, the water managed intimately and daily by pumps and dykes and canals. So much philosophy about what is real and what is artificial springs from this everyday fact that every conversation in the Netherlands carries profundity as a spice. The important distinction that day, with Katrina, is that what we call the real world, the hard place in which imagination and hope are not enough, the world of laws and mortgages and society and what you need to know to sustain your way of life, is itself artificial. What you might think of as the real world, that of the Earth and the planets and wilderness and life and death and the origin of species and what you need to know to survive is something else again; the *actual world* Katrina calls it. The real world is but a part – the human part – of the actual world.

The whine of a jumbo jet above makes me crane my neck to

watch it. I catch it just as the wheels came down ready for the run into landing at Schipol and the pilot races the engines a little to compensate for the drag.

"If you said your life was like an airline flight, now, that might have some balls," says Katrina. It brings me back to the moment. What?

"An airline flight: there's so much techno wizardry in that process – just like life now – and so much sitting around waiting for the next thing to happen – like life now – not to mention the security cameras, the regulated behaviour, the precise weight and contents of your belongings being an issue: and the passports, the ID cards! They mean you're guilty unless you can prove yourself innocent! Air travel is just like modern life!"

Remember, all this was prompted by me saying that life is like standing on the back of a ship watching your ignorance disappear over the horizon. "Ships are all colonisation and fate and women and children first:" says Katrina, "old fashioned! Airplanes are keeping your seat belt fastened and fuel burn rates and movies repeated every two hours and deep vein thromboses: contemporary!"

And what's more, she says, "you English, how does that slogan go? *Born British, English by the grace of God!* No wonder you're all so sentimental!" Oof!

Why do I love her so much, when she says things like that? I first saw Katrina thumping through the park in jogging shoes, glistening all over with sweat, arms pumping, aerobic breathing, tight T shirt with *STOP STARING AT MY BREASTS!* printed across her chest in big letters – I thought she was Venus emerging from the ocean. That night in a restaurant we watched a man ask his woman to marry him Hollywood style, on one knee with a ring in a little velvet box and the whole place watching, waiting to applaud when she said yes – Katrina jumped up and said to me, "down on your knees! Repeat after me! My darling Katrina!" *My darling Katrina.* "Will you do me the honour!" *Will you do me the honour.* "Of becoming my fuck-buddy!"

The airliner is now so close we can see the gorgeous heraldic colours of the airline against the thunderous cloudscape. It is December, and the gulls have moved back into the city, screeching and swooping across the sky at the same time, and suddenly the analogy of life-as-flying makes a different sense. The landing of the airliner – one way or another, whether safely on wheels or broken to bits in a crash – is implicit in the take off. No drifting across the ocean is possible, no abandoning ship; no maybe or perhaps or let's try it this way – a flight is a commitment; it's a commitment like being born is. And while babies are all thrust and push, heading for that burst of sunshine up there beyond the clouds of adolescence, oldsters are all final glide slope, locked onto their final beacons, throttled back and falling out of the sky, buffeted by crosswinds on their way to the terminal.

"For heaven's sake!" Says Katrina. "You can't stop, can you? Who are you, bloody Bill Clinton?" Oof!

AS WE GET OFF THE FERRY a big black Audi hammers across the tramlines and pulls up across the cycle lane with a double thump. No one drives a big car in Amsterdam; there's nowhere to leave it. Except where this guy leaves it. Immediately a jam of cyclists and pedestrians trying to squeeze past the car builds up and I am just about to contribute a few cents to the chorus of complaints when Katrina spins round and kisses me quick and mouths regret and spins again and runs towards the car, and the door swings open and she climbs into it. All legs and nose and hair, my beautiful Katrina. She flashes a smile as they roar off. I catch a glimpse of the driver and his mouthful of teeth and he looks to me ninety five percent gangster. No, make that ninety five percent pimp. He looks like a pimp!

5

Public Space

Back at home in my canal side studio, emails are incoming. My American friend Kevin, who gets a million emails a day, has his Mac set to go "uh-oh" every time one arrives. He sits there surrounded by the welter of his busy life with uh-oh, uh-oh, uh-oh punctuating the background like a whole committee of grandpas. My life by the canal is a lot less busy, but here is an invitation to write about Public Space and Public Art from the grandly named *Podium voor Architectuur Haarlemmermeer en Schipol*. I am concerned about the Dutch translation – who will do it? Oh we all speak English here, no problem, is the answer. But as a Dutchman said to me the other day, "Yeah, we all speak it, sure. Everyone in the world does. But you know what? In ten years time no one will understand you but they will understand me because I speak World English!" Meaning that a native English speaker's use of idiom and implication is "just too fucking dense" as he put it. In reality what the rest of the world speaks is American, and that's what the Lingua Franca is, pidgin American. But still – Public Space, Public Art. What a great subject for someone dwelling on *How To Like Everything*. Public Space is where the value of everything becomes mutual, not just personal. Public space is where everything used to happen, from markets to festivals to executions. Maybe *How To Like Everything* can be thrashed out like a tribal pecking order is thrashed out, in public space. As a function of public space. And there, outside, bright in the morning sunshine, is the place I can use as illustration. The public square in front of the Oude Kerk. I can see it all from the window.

But it doesn't turn out like that. Writing begins with an image that coalesces into a sentence and then grows more images and more sentences as if by electrolysis. Gradually I lose sight of the Old Church and find myself thinking about Trafalgar Square, London, England, the home of Nelson and his big bronze lions. The anode for the process is the statues that fill the place, and the cathode the dreams of a lost empire:

The landscape of the city of London, as everyone knows, I start to type, *is made of set pieces. There is Piccadilly Circus, with its aluminium statue of Eros, god of love. There's the traffic circle outside the palace, with its huge monolith of Queen Victoria sitting on top of her empire, represented by the lion of Africa and the elephant of India. And there's Trafalgar Square, with Horatio Nelson standing, one eyed, one armed, on top of his column.* I have to stop and think why it is like this, this ambience I take for granted as a Londoner born and bred: *The themes are loud and clear. Destiny, empire and war – they are the British passions of a hundred years ago, played out by allegory in the public realm.*

A little way east from Trafalgar Square down The Strand, opposite Charing Cross station, is Zimbabwe House. The building was built in 1908, in the time of the cubists, but is a four-square stone banker's pile just as you would expect in that part of the world except that, in the spirit of the new century, high up on the façade, is a series of statues made by Jacob Epstein, who left no stone unturned in his search for controversy. The statues are figures representing motherhood, manliness and beauty – but manifested in such a brutal and materialistic spirit that they became the subject of fury the moment they were unveiled. People hated them. Young men took their mothers on detours to escape them. Fathers shielded the eyes of their daughters as they passed. For thirty years they epitomized a new idea, not that public art is the summing up of a community's aspirations, but that public art is a public nuisance! Until at last the building was sold and the new owners went out there with hammers and knocked the breasts and genitals off the statues. They knocked off the faces too, while they were at it. It's all still there, this mutilation. The official explanation is that the statues were unsafe. And when you look at the building today, you think it must be war damage. But no: it's public art, public nuisance.

And, thinking about that, I find myself writing this: *After a century of breakdown, the public realm has tiptoed indoors and turned on the television, where it can tune in to its own passions, its invasions of privacy, its poems to shampoo and its circus of famous fleas.*

ALL THIS TIME THE OUTSIDE WORLD is still tapping on my head waiting to be let in. Outside my window is the quiet morning presence of the church square. If I look over to the right I can see through the naked branches of the trees the shop front of the whore who sits there all day in what seems to be old lady's underwear brushing her waist length hair. She is a success. Something in the set up draws the punters in, they pass and re-pass twice and then – look, here's one: he sidles up to the door and whispers the sweet nothings of money to her and disappears inside. She draws the curtain and fifteen minutes later draws it open again and he reappears in the world slowly spinning to a stop like an ejected CD.

If I look over to the left there is the brick paved apron in front of the church, which would make a good place for burning someone at the stake. Given a sixty-metre buffer zone for a really good, hot fire, I reckon you could pack five hundred people in to this little square. It probably happened there, too, when the Spanish whipped through Holland in a tsunami of horror, cutting the hands off children and stringing men up by the testicles. Four hundred and sixty years ago. Is that a lot or a little? I once had a plan to write a history of England where the story of his life was told by a man of eighty-five to a child of five; who then grew up and old and at age eighty five told the story of his life to another five year old child, who then grew up, etcetera: You need but twelve lives, twelve chunks of eighty years, to cover the whole history of England from the Norman conquest to the present day. Six lives will take you back to sit in at the first night of Hamlet; or to witness at first hand those atrocities in the Spanish Netherlands.

But right now in the peace of the present moment there is the beauty of the old building with its gilded carvings in the crisp winter sunshine and its fringe of bicycles, and tourists standing on the bridge and pulling out little cameras to snap the view of the ancient warehouses up the old canal with the spire of the catholic church sticking up behind them. Hundreds of people snap this self same view everyday; and so the public space of Oudekerksplein is promulgated widely. How would you frame that picture taking – is it public art? Is it some sort of parallel to the public debates we have about our city spaces and what to do with them? So that instead of statues commemorating great men, we have a million images commemorating democratic debate?

And is it not the artists that make art? Well, no: criticism is now the substance of art making to such a degree that many of today's public artists do away with the product as an issue, and make public debate the contents of their art. In doing so they are not redefining art so much as redefining public space. The debate itself has become the public space.

I wonder if the statues will ever recover their lost grounds, and how long the current phase of public space by computer and mobile phone – telepathic space – will maintain. I think of that fourth plinth in Trafalgar Square that no one could decide what to do with so they chose a thousand people at random and set them up on the plinth in rotation and called it people's art. The acts featured on the plinth were inconsequential – I saw one man who had collected a bag of conkers and painted numbers on them and was tossing them into the crowd like a man feeding bears at the zoo. The real story was in the plinth itself. To stop this man and all the others hurting themselves a huge safety net supported on steel beams and painted grey like the ones they have on aircraft carriers to catch overshooting planes was attached to the plinth. I think that was the real sculpture, that net. It was made out of the problem of democracy – which is that it starts out as the means of collective action against oppression and then abruptly runs out of steam. Democracy has no value in itself, it is made of the will of the majority, whatever that is at the time. It is a way of dealing with everything, but it is a utility, not a vision. To think of it as a vision results in a thousand regulations surrounding every action, because ultimately democracy depends on the law. That safety net was an example of the *art of the law*.

As I watch out of my window and muse and think all this, a big black Audi noses its way into the little square across the canal and squeezes through the tourists right up onto the narrow bridge and stops. And parks! Right there! And out climbs the same man who took Katrina away back at the Ferry terminal. What is he doing here? And how does he get away with parking that big car right there? The only other vehicle I've ever seen stop on that bridge was a police van, which turned up hooting its nee-nors one night and bundled an entire stag party inside and took off again like Thunderbird 2. I stretch to get a better view, rubbernecking like a rodent, and watch hypnotized as the man's gaze swivels across the ground like a searchlight and lifts slowly up the wall of the house to stare straight at me.

Two other men - I recognize them, as well, now I think of it, they're always standing around here somewhere, approach the car from opposite sides of the square and exchange elaborate fist-hammer handshakes with him and hand over packages to him that look like bundles of cash. I slink back behind the curtain as he looks back up at my window and shafts a big smile at me and raises his hand. Holy cow! He knows where I live!

6

The Pack of Thoughts

The objects making public space, the statues and buildings, are *specific to the homonidae*, Michel Serres – the maverick of French letters – writes in *Genesis*, and they stabilize our relationships and slow down the intervals of revolution. Not so for the other primates. *For an unstable band of baboons*, he goes on, *social changes are flaring up every minute. One could characterize their history as unbound, insanely so.*

I once watched a movie that followed the events and tribulations of two tribes of baboons in Africa. They were Anubis baboons, whose adult males have huge manes of thick hair and canine teeth like swords. They live in big packs – not like wolves, in dozens, but in troops of several hundred. The hierarchies in these packs are delineated as strictly as if Dickens had written them, and as I was watching the movie curled up with Jackie and his mum on our big red sofa, the sight of the animals ranged across their browsing grounds like citizens woven into a social fabric raised strong feelings for the commonality of primate life in all of us.

Especially this: the movie concentrated on the antics of a young female baboon, a favourite daughter of the alpha male, who spent what time he had left over from copulation prowling the edges of the terrain watching out for trouble. This little princess scampered about doing whatever the hell she felt like and no one was allowed to stop her. At one point she clambers onto the lap of an elderly female who's peacefully peeling and eating fruit and starts picking the pieces out of the old one's fingers and stuffing them in her own mouth. Sitting there, brazenly chewing, spoilt rotten. If that happened to you, you would sweep the little one off your lap with a snarl and a hiss, but the old one can't do that: alpha male, way across the other side of the troop, is watching. So she gathers up what's left of the fruit and puts it all in her mouth at once and clenches it tight shut and the little princess starts in pulling at her old lips and prizing them apart and poking at her old teeth to try and get two fingers inside her mouth, which stays clamped closed, her head straining back as far as she can, fury in her eyes and, I'll bet, murder in her heart. This shocking display of privilege abused is so *Marie Antoinette* that the three of us sitting on the sofa couldn't wait for the revolution to happen. And sure enough, it arrived in the shape of two burly young males with brand new manes and charismatic muscles who ganged together to overcome the alpha. There was a big scuffle that seemed to kick up all the brown dust of Africa, but before too long they had him on the ground. He retired immediately and went to sit in a tree while the two deposers beta-and-gamma'd the daylights out of each other until there was only one left standing.

This is not quite revolution as humans know it, although the character of a joint action that quickly splits into factions is what does happen with us. *Coups d'etat* are a regularity in baboon life. They do it instead of holding elections. And the aftermath is generally peaceful. The reality of alpha leadership is that the Alpha male gets to do most of the insemination while he's in office, so a lot of the tribe are descended from him, hence are related to each other, hence the established relationships in the tribe will maintain. Which makes me think: is that why a Scottish clan chief was called 'father' of the clan – because he literally was? Was feudal life back then as much a family life as the baboons'?

Anyway: the very first act of the new leadership is to chase that obnoxious little princess clear out of the community. The movie shows her little pink bum scuttling off down into the valley swatted and spat at by everyone she passes, and it follows her on her subsequent wanderings as she tries to join another tribe – and has to start right over, right at the bottom of the pecking order.

THE NEXT DAY I am walking through public space dodging the bikes and gawping at the breasts of the women for hire, and I haven't gone more than fifty metres before I hear a deep voice behind me.

"Hey, man, I know where you live." It says. I turn, to see the man with the Audi standing there with an *I am the alpha and omega* expression on his face. Then he cracks a smile: "Isn't that what the bad guy says?" He pushes his hand towards me and says his name is Bamba. Bamba! And then, as I continue walking, he falls in beside me and starts to talk. I assume he wants to find out how much I saw back there on the bridge, but no – it seems to be just chat. Pleasantry. As we pass the sex shop on Oudeverburgwaal he points out an artificial vagina in the window and tells me it's "modelled on the actual interior" of a specific porn star. So next I think it's going to be about Katrina – she of the Anubis profile – but no, as we pass the lurid transvestite display in the shop window on the corner of Molensteeg, he tells me he wishes he had a "real education" like me.

"I can make people do what I want," he says. "I know how to feed the animals in the donkey sanctuary. But you, I mean guys like you, you need to give something back to the world, because you have the power."

"There is knowledge, and there is what you know." I say. By which I mean that *knowledge* is the letters after your name. *Knowing* is what got into your head through experience. I am paraphrasing Gertrude Stein. For whom there was no qualification that mattered more than feeling.

"See! That's what I mean. *There is knowledge and there's what you know*. That's so great."

So great? And so easy to say. I try to explain what it means to me: usually books of knowledge are criss-crossed with blizzards of footnotes referring to the other volumes that contribute to their field – without this corroboration, they intone, how can what you know be trusted? Whereas I –

"There you go, babes!" He says, interrupting me with a playful punch.

We pass the little pack of crackheads who inhabit the corner of Oude Hoogstraat and the Klovenier canal. They look like the beggars in nursery rhymes from two hundred years ago. They usually come up to me in their smelly rags and try and score money, especially when I'm with Jackie, but when they see who I'm with this time they slink back into shelter. Okay. I decide to tell him something complicated, about the problems for choirs singing Rachmaninov's vespers. It's a story about the dynamics of everyday relativity. In unaccompanied choral music, especially with a large choir, there is a tendency for the music to drift flat as it progresses. The change is inaudible to the participants or the audience, who are caught in the relational web of the moment. In Rachmaninov's vespers, however, the bass lines are notoriously at the bottom of the register of most singers – in the Nunc Dimittis they reach the B flat below low C – and so as the choir tends towards the flat, pressure is put on the basses trying to flex with the tuning. They reach a sort of human absolute of low voicedness.

"Wow!" he says. "I'm gonna use that one!" and I think, how are you going to use that? You gonna write my book? And somehow he knows what I'm thinking, because he laughs a big laugh and slaps me on the back. "Don't worry!" He says. "You worry too much, man!"

BIOLOGISTS TELL US that individuals in shoals and flocks manage their progress by continuously monitoring the few others immediately adjacent to them. This is how those big flocks of starlings that appear in central Europe in the fall pull off their spectacular swooping cloud formations. At home on my desk is a well thumbed copy of *A Thousand Plateaus* by the great mentors of multiplicity Gilles Deleuze and Felix Guattari, a book that is way too radical to be compared to Bamba, but somehow has Bamba's same brand of bumptious assertion. It says this about life in packs: animals that live in nomadic packs live outside the stasis of laws and territories. This is most complicated in mammal packs, for here the dominant and submissive behaviours endemic to all societies – even bees bully each other, apparently – erupt into the sort of leadership spats we saw in the baboons. The leaders of these fluid organisations cannot rely on precedent or law, since everything – everyone – is always shifting. They need practical cunning. As Deleuze and Guattari put it, *the leader has to gamble everything on every move.* Now what I'm thinking is that I am the leader of a pack of thoughts, the pack of likes and dislikes that populates my head. This pack is continuously shifting, things on the periphery becoming central, things in the middle flying to the edge; if I want to like everything I must let the pack shift and self organize, I must not burden it with structure but follow the flow, and gamble on a positive outcome. I must do the opposite of what we are taught to do all our lives. Remember those six degrees of separation? Those six historical lives? Look: Celine Dion, Mariah Carey, Beyonce, Alicia Keys, Lauryn Hill, Erykha Badu. Did you see what happened there? Context is everything. Isn't it a whole lot better than saying *oh god! Celine Dion! I can't stand her!*

And now Bamba and I have come all the way down to the Dam of Amster-Dam, which is the big public space of the centre city, and we find the place full of commotion and noise and hundreds of men dressed in red and white clothes. Football supporters. Ajax is playing Feyenoord this afternoon and the home crowd is out in force. The rivalry between Amsterdam and Rotterdam is keen and hard. They have painted their faces and are wearing archaic red and white jokers' hats with long felt spikes carrying bells, and they push and shove as though they own the place. And right now, they do. The noise is tremendous. I yell over it and tell Bamba the macabre story about Dutch settlers in seventeenth century New Amsterdam, now New York, who played football one day on Broadway with the heads of some natives they had massacred. The strife engendered by this barbarity is what caused the wall on Wall Street to be built, and what kicked off an escalation in hostility that never slowed until all the native tribes of America had been concentrated into reservations almost three hundred years later: and I wonder whether that noise the crowd is making, a sound that swells and swoops abruptly like a flock of birds, only with menace rather than beauty, is the same as on that day in the new world.

As I stand in the soccer crowd and it fluxes and spins round its changing centres, I ask myself if this sort of thing could be classed as debate. Question: what shall we do with public space? Answer: this! It is a historic space, a space made of rumour and flux, an Anabaptist space, a witch hunter's space, a public execution sort of space. I stand in the middle of the turbulence asking, "but can we still have statues, please?" And then Bamba suddenly breaks into a run and disappears into the throng, swallowed up as spray is by the waves.

DOWN BY THE OLD HARBOUR, where blocks of apartments are going up in the *SuperDutch* style, a brusque hand-over-fist in blue - KLM - and orange - national soccer strip - and grey - the colour of machines, a stone sculpture stands. It is a solid block of limestone, a three-metre cube, covered in what look like the scratches of wild beasts. Several stone carving chisels and hammers are attached to it by chains silently inviting passers by to contribute to the evolving shape of the thing; which they do – although if you've tried stone carving, you'll know that the implacability of the material asserts itself immediately on the beginner. This is why start-up classes in stone carving all end up with a bunch of tortoises, like ashtrays used to in school pottery classes. And that is why this democratic sculpture is covered in scratches, and is slowly taking on a completely different aspect of victory to Nelson's column: the aspect of attempts on its nature repelled.

The debate itself has become the public space. This in itself is an exciting state of affairs, and may see the current generation through. And it may be enough to leave it there. But is there any future for the product? Do those who love the material of public art, the columns and plinths and giant statues, have anything to look forward to?

Maybe this: it is a quality of contemporary fragmentation that works of art have the potential to escape their valuation, and run outside those busily debated narratives. It would be a loose and wild existence, but art in such a free fall could at last let go of its critiques, and become instead the perception of things yet unnamed.

And public space? Public space would be everywhere.

Angeland

"Here is the news," say the angels. It is cold here in Angeland, and they've wrapped their nakedness in feathers. In the background there is the faint hiss of the cosmic radiation, an echo of the big bang still audible fourteen billion years after the event. They speak again: "Here is the news. Governments today ratified stage two of the trade treaty in which carbon emissions worldwide will be cut in half by the middle of the century. The chorus of Prime Ministers, seen here standing in the hall of mirrors in the palace of palaces where the armistice that ended the war of the worlds was signed, said that this undertaking will cost trillions of billions, and taxes will rise world wide as carbon emissions fall. But that we have no other choice."

Huh? Why?!!! Why should reducing something cost more? Why doesn't burning less fuel cost less? If we all stopped wanting stuff and gave up our jobs and spent our time growing food in the streets and singing and dancing, zero carbon would cost nothing!

The difference between you and us," say the angels, "is that we believe in Progress, and you don't." They explain, with the patience of ages, that my zero-carbon hippy-Native-American primitivist fantasy would be dominated by inequalities and tribal pecking order strife – because human nature itself does not progress. In fact Progress is not something you ever attain, it's something you have to continually strive for. Eliminating poverty, bringing healthcare to the underclass, extending opportunity to everyone, even just being equal: it all costs money. It all takes a lot of work. "We're not talking about using less energy, we're talking about using more but shifting the mode to sustainable, so we can keep the program rolling," they say. In other words, it's not the saving of the planet that costs a packet, it's the progress. "Let us pray," they say. Do we pray instead of singing and dancing? "That's right." And when I ask how do I pray? They say, "you work – prayer is work."

And it's only several years later, as I wipe the sweat off my brow with my aching muscles, that a second question occurs to me – huh? Why?!!! Why should we need to progress? Why should we have to work so hard to correct suffering? Why is the world so full of suffering in the first place?

The angels have a story about this too, and everyone knows it. The cast of characters is god and the devil and Adam and Eve and a snake, the setting is a garden, the prop is an apple and the narrative is of disaster. Everyone knows that the snake is temptation and that the forbidden apple is the taste of the knowledge of good and evil. The grace the first two humans lost – in this story – was their innocence about the world. They had been told not to touch, but they did; and as punishment they were flung out of the Garden of Eden into the wilderness and the place was shut up with a fence of flaming swords. That's what it says in the bible.

Which prompts another question. What happened to the Garden of Eden? Why can't we find the remains of it? It was lost in the deluge, you say?

There is an ancient post-Christ heresy, fermented in the deserts of Egypt in the three or four hundred years before Rome got a grip on Christianity, that tries to answer those questions. Adam and Eve Two. It has the same characters and events as Adam and Eve One but a completely reversed emphasis. The story tells that the world and all the forms of life inside it were made not by god but by the devil. He called it hell. His mischievous intent was to trap the spiritual in material form, so that suffering, the troublesome, difficult suffering of the flesh, would prevail. And the serpent was sent not by the devil but by god. Its mission was to make Adam and Eve aware of their plight, to give them the knowledge of good and evil, because they needed to know that the material world they were trapped in was the devil's realm. When the devil discovered what had happened he flew into a rage and smashed up the garden. We don't need to look for the Garden of Eden because it's right here; we still live in it today. It is a broken world of ice and deserts and tempests, hostile and full of suffering – it is still the devil's realm – it is hell. This version of the story tells us we are now in hell. And how do we get out? Well, there the answer is the same as in Adam and Eve One. We have to pray. Non-stop.

Lola came in to the room just now and looked at my notes – A+E 1 progress, A+E 2 heresy. "A and E? Are you writing about hospitals now?" What? "A and E – Accident and Emergency." She said. When I explained what I was doing she said it was funny that Adam, the man, should be the Accident and Eve, the woman, the Emergency. And then she sat down in the other chair and told me, apropos paradise and angels, about Milan Kundera's idea about angels. She called him "Milan 'Unbearable Lightness of Being' Kundera". She said that he says that the angels are not on the side of goodness; they're on the side of God's creation. It's not the same thing. "They are pretty stern. If you don't fall into line, they'll send you to the Gulag."

I don't want to go the Gulag and I don't want to fall into line. You would think science and reason had put an end to speculations about lost paradise and broken worlds. You would think that the revolutions in thinking and action over the last five hundred years would have scotched such creationist nonsense forever. But the story persists. It's not just that everyone knows it, everyone still believes it. Uses it on a daily basis to explain the world. The current version of the Garden of Eden story is that the world was once a green and perfect place, where everything lived in a delicate ecological balance. Until humans came into the world and bent it to their will. Using fire and machines, they turned the earth inside out, they paved over paradise, they upset the harmony of nature and will not cease even now the world is broken and the climate itself is becoming furious and hostile. What can we do? We must strive to correct the folly. We must work and pay out billions. And pray? Yes! Pray that it's not too late.

So here we stand in a world that we think needs mending, that we find as full of suffering as it is of splendour – for all we know it could be the devil's domain. We think we are like A + E fallen from paradise. We think the suffering is our fault and so we strive to progress, to heal the world and make it better.

Lola says I've left something out: the problem of evolution being taught as though it were a creation story. She means that both creation and evolution are given as descriptions of the orderly descent of the current world. "You would think from all the sound and fury that creation and evolution were opposites, but they're not! They're both creation stories!" She says. The creation story describes the way things are and the fall story describes why humans are in such a state about the way things are. So if evolution is a creation story, what's the evolution fall story? Emergence? Is that what the actual world is?

If Charles 'Origin of Species' Darwin had not been himself a deist, he might have used that word emergence rather than 'origin' in the title of his book. Emergence was minted in a later extension of evolutionary theory made by biologists in an attempt to account for the appearance, through evolutionary processes, of new phenomena. Specifically, the appearance of human consciousness, which, they said, has no apparent precedent in the natural world. It was even speculated by some philosophers, learning from Einstein's relativity, that emergence might one day produce what could only be called god. I refer to the work of Samuel Alexander, in Space, Time and Deity, written in 1920 and presaging the growth in metaphysics that has resurfaced in philosophy now the long battle with mathematics has been lost: in which he posits the emergence through evolution of a higher consciousness with which the remaining mysteries will be unfurled, an intelligence as distant from ours as ours is from the bacteria in our guts.

How about that? God does not yet exist, but will evolve to exist in the future. The holy books tell us that man was made in his image. But this is a different perception. We came first. We are the creative ones, we make the babies and we make the other worlds – and the god we have, god the creator of all things, is something else we have made. Something we have made in our image.

3
Narratives

Think about how you create if you do create you do not remember yourself as you do create. And yet time and identity is what you tell about as you create only while you create they do not exist.
Gertrude Stein, *What Are Masterpieces and Why There Are So Few Of Them*

7

Clichés

The winter is really coming on now. In the last cold snap I said to the butcher on the corner, a big guy with blood red hands, purveyor of meat to whores and pimps: "Cold today, huh?" stamping my feet and rubbing my hands together. "Hey, you wait until winter comes," he said. It was the middle of January, and I thought he was making a joke. But now, here it is. The ice on the canal is thick enough to skate on and snow is backed up everywhere. People skid about on their bikes on the slippery streets. When you go out, bundled up in scarves and hats, the cold wind attacks your eyes and yanks tears out of them and then tries to freeze the tears. It could be a love story, this weather.

And here crunching through the snow clutching the handlebars of his bike is my colleague from the art school, Fronk. His hands are raw in the cold, showing red, white and blue, skin, knuckles and veins. He never wears gloves. He is famous amongst his friends for being hard. He is an architect, so he is given to conclusive statements. Architects don't equivocate because they work with the material world every day – at least that's what they should be doing, according to Fronk. Never mind that they spend half their time schmoozing and elbowing others out of the way – and he's off on his hobbyhorse already. Here comes his line on culture – "nothing but a cult!" he says, "listen to the word. That's all it is." His face flushes when he says these things, and his eyes pop. He gets angry at the drop of a pin. He despises the celebrated buildings of the SuperDutch that swoop and curve "like the gestures flung out of car windows in heavy traffic." He says such buildings are not even architecture, they are culture. And spits on the ground. What is he, a traditionalist? No. A modernist, then? No. He is not any ist. He is an architect whose buildings are as serious as the bricks they are made of and that is all. *That is all* is the whole point.

"A brick is a brick is a brick is a brick," Fronk once said to me. He says that a building is to a city as a brick is to a brick wall; essential, but unremarkable. And that is all. Could *that is all* be another way of saying *that is everything*? No, says Fronk: because 'everything' is 'culture'. It's no use arguing with him. He thinks that contemporary culture is revisionist, the modern life version of tradition, which translates tradition's ossified practices and love of the old into shifting custom and infatuation with the new. Now I agree with him on that – but I like it. I also like Fronk's built like a brick shit-house constructions, which are as busy doing without tradition as they are doing without culture. Much to his disgust, I like it all.

This morning his face seems to be a harder red than usual. I am glad to see him because I have something to ask him. I want to discuss why things are different from each other. It's a simple question, maybe for Fronk a stupid one, but it's been dogging me. Is it because of the old cliché of form following function? And is that like or not like saying giraffes need long necks so they get them? Or is the form of things entirely arbitrary, spinning out the chance mutations of DNA in the biomass, or of human choices in the real world? Fronk is unmoved by my questions. He looks at me like a dumb animal, not like him at all. I take him by the ring in his nose and steer him into the cafe at the top of the harbour building, eleven floors up, which has a view right across the city. You can see all the way to Haarlem, twenty kilometres away, from up there. The vertigo by itself is exciting, let alone the hint you get of the curvature of the earth. And Fronk? All the way up in the elevator he stares at the floor. I'm talking to myself. I'll have to do *form and function* by myself.

The sequence of function following form is an old one, all tied up with the modern anxiety about the superficiality of style. But Gregory Bateson, the information theory anthropologist, had a different twist on it back in the nineteen seventies. In his book *Mind and Nature* he drew attention to the interdependence of form and function. He said that biological forms are held in code in DNA, instructions that he characterized as digital. The bodies that grow from the instructions, which he describes as functions, are the analogues. You are a function of your DNA. But which comes first? Digital or analogue? And why does this sound as if, contrary to modernist cliché, that function follows form? The answer is that neither comes first. Your body, shaped by its code, is also the torch carrier of that code. The form of DNA must be embedded in its function to survive, so function and form determine each other. There may indeed be a sequence: form follows function follows form follows function follows form. And more than this, since DNA mutations are arbitrary, form is arbitrary too!

Fronk sits across the table on the crowded terrace, unmoved by my revelations but looking like the perfect storm. I try again to jolt a reaction. I say that I'm beginning to like clichés. I'm beginning to realise that they are a sort of pidgin philosophy that we all use as we motor through the trials of life. They help us without us having to stop and think. Like prejudice. Like common sense, I suppose. Are prejudice and cliché good things? What do you say, Fronk?

"You know Katrina has a new lover?" Is what he says. "Don't misunderstand, I don't mind lovers, there can't be too much love in the world. But she thinks he is so great, her *outlaw*. She thinks he is *underground*. She thinks he is *alternative*." The three words in italics are spat, not spoken.

The special thing about Fronk is that Katrina is in fact married to *him*. The openness of their marriage is outstanding to all of us because it is so old fashioned. So nineteen-thirties. Open marriages are like totalitarian states. They have contradictory ethics. *So long as I don't know* is one. *So long as you don't fall in love with anyone else* is another.

"So long as she stays out of trouble, okay?" Says Fronk. "But this man is no good. He's dangerous for her. Does he think Katrina's one of his whores? If he makes trouble, I'll trouble him!" Thumping the table and making the glasses rattle and the puddles of beer shiver and the other Amsterdammers sitting all around us stare. How to like one thing and *that is all* – where *all* means *everything* – does have clarity on its side. But that's what's dangerous here. And today's all and everything for Fronk is Katrina.

SO FAR in searching for how to like everything I've heard the claims of the evangelists, and the claims of the doctors, I've listened to the pimp's eye view, I've bumped across public space. I've recalled the discrimination and the clarities of youth – and now I understand that how to like everything is not a critical project. Katrina is a Critical Theorist, dedicated to plumbing the culture for its contradictions and trying to unravel them in the interest of making a better world. For her, alternative and underground are critical positions. Fronk, her contradictory espoused, is a Critical Realist, which is different. He is dedicated to cleaving the material world from the soup of impressions in our heads. But he is still pursuant of a better world. Neither Katrina nor Frank, in between disagreeing with each other, will agree with me that there is no possibility of a better world. Never mind how much I point to the derelict social programs that fringe our cities, the collapsed revolutions that populate our histories, the corrupted hopes of technologies whose consequences we must now deal with; *they just got it wrong*, they both say from their opposite ends of the critical spectrum. *We must be critical, and then we can try again*, they say.

But How To Like Everything is not critical. It takes the world as multi focused and negotiates understanding. It exercises judgement, but is not judgemental. This is why the double meaning of 'discriminate' is so striking; and now I'm thinking that prejudice and cliché are the critical language of common sense, can I revive them as positives? I remember something about primitive painting. That school of amateurs who are precisely not schooled, *who paint not what they see but what they know*, in the words of Fairfield Porter the sixties American painter and art thinker. He goes on: *A primitive accepts prejudice, and this decision in advance is what produces the shock and surprise. The conceptual clarity does not reproduce appearances but competes with them, and this is why the appearance of primitive painting is brighter than nature.*

This is another sort of clarity and one I need to run past Katrina; thinking of whom with Fronk glowering in the background makes me remember that *all the nice girls love an outlaw*. A cliché about the thrill of living on the edge. *The edge*: that's a cliché too. How many hours a week do you spend watching soaps about murder and revenge and illegitimacy, about gangsters and pimps? Why are such lives worth writing about? It's because they imply a critique of bourgeois society. And this alternative has now become the mainstream. The mode of the anti-hero is embedded in contemporary culture. So much so that my simple project – How to Like Everything – requires me to pull on crampons daily to climb the mountains of criticism, the heaps of not-liking-everything piled up outside the front door.

8

Special-Not-Special

It's a new day. It's up in the morning and out to school. I take Jackie's hands and introduce them to the sleeves of his coat and he pulls his gloves on *all by himself,* and holds them up with his thumbs crammed into the little fingers. We head out onto the frosted streets of the city. Into one of those fine clear winter mornings where the contrails of passing airliners on their way to Singapore and New York criss cross the sky with artificial clouds. Like glaciers in Iceland, clear blue skies in Northern Europe are becoming a thing of the past. But the church clocks keep chiming, and there's ice on the canals.

We stop at the herring stall on the bridge to get breakfast and my unusual boy slips the oily fillets down his throat so readily that the fish man behind the counter says, "There's a boy who can eat!" and, holding up his ruddy hand to Jackie, "high five!" The cold day coils our breaths into steam and Jackie barks smoke signals at the gulls lurking round the stall just like he used to at the pigeons back home in London. He thinks there is nothing better than tearing into a flock of landed birds and shooing them to flight, grey pigeons, white seagulls, black crows; they're all fun. They all do it so differently. The pigeons wait till the last second and go off like an explosion, the crows look as though they can't believe you're really going to do it, hopping a leggy retreat before jumping into the air and catching themselves on their huge black wings. And these Dutch ducks! In Amsterdam they squat by the side of the canals until Jackie comes hooting up and then just jump off the wall into the water two metres below like serial suicides; and in the splashing commotion his face lights up again with delight as it does a thousand times a day.

And so we travel, stopping and hooting and dashing and

shooing, until we turn the last corner and there is the school with its jam of bicycles; and the milling parents, and the hoots of the children meeting up with their friends.

This school of Jackie's is what's called a *special school*. 'Special' means 'not like the rest of us'. Complicated, because the word comes from the same root as the word *species*, which distinguishes one kind of being from another. So special means *different in kind*. It can also mean exceptional; out of the ordinary. Except that the implication delivered in *special school* is that *not like the rest of us* is not a good way to be. Or, to put it the straight way – *just like the rest of us* is the best way to be.

It is left to the parents of special children to rage against this discrimination, which is given a further twist in the clubs and cliques that claim distinction when they describe those outside the club as *not one of us*. We are not like the rest of them – we are *special*, they say! So that when it comes to schools, which preserve their distinctions from each other in performance league-tables so rarefied that children like Trogo can never keep up, they find that he is *special-not-special*, not only *not one of us* but also *not one of them*. By the time the *special-not-specials* have clattered through the slots of the machine and into the reject tray, you have a distillation of the unteacheable of the herd. You can glimpse there the stupidity of what William Blake called the *Satanic mills*. He imagined the academies of his day as machines that separated out the spirit from the material like a mill separates kernel from husk, and although I am thinking of a different kind of separation, the metaphor holds because the ever-tightening standards in schools means an ever-narrowing path to success, which means an ever-growing group of excludeds that have to be managed in special ways. I think you would call that process Satanic, if you could conceive of a secular Satan.

So we parents invent our own ways of carrying on. Some feel they have been chosen by god for the difficult task of raising a special child. Some spend all their time on the Internet looking for cures, some spend all their money looking for justice from the law. My way is to rant against the conformity that excludes the special. It helps to be writing a book called *How To Like Everything*. And in the background for all of us, maybe because of the way the genome project and the possibility of cloning is driving the popular imagination and its craving for origin stories to believe that *everything* is genetic – we feel that it's possible that all our children's problems may have been inherited from us. What a strife torn collection we are!

THE BEAUTY OF THE CHILDREN THEMSELVES is that they are beyond such quarrels. Along with all their other oblivions, they are oblivious to discrimination. Earlier I said that children are not innocent but ignorant; meaning that they are adding to their experience of the real world and its complex social contracts every minute of every day. This bunch of Jackie's don't progress like that. They maintain something like an actual innocent state. I think that's why they scare people so much. What it adds up to is a strange kind of freedom: freedom from peer pressure, freedom from expectation. Freedom from the uniform that normal children – we call normal children *neurotypicals* – so happily put on. Our children will never be soldiers. They may turn out to be killers, but they won't kill on somebody else's orders.

Lola, who stares reality harder in the face than I do, is not so sure. She tells a story about meeting some disaware – unknowingly ignorant – adult when she was out with Jacko who asked "and what do you want to be when you grow up?" Met with silence, he carries on "Oh! I see! Not talking to me, eh?" Which is what they always say to cover their embarrassment. And Lola suddenly thought, thought this about her own son: *he could always be a torturer. He certainly has the detachment for it.*

Torturers? Are they special? Damn. How do you like that?

The uniqueness of a person, of every person, confounds the

idea of normal. We all know that. But if that can be so, so it could be with everything that there is. There is no ordinary, there is no everyday. There is no curriculum for learning about life – there is simply knowledge and there is what you know. The experience of caring for Jackie has shown me a working model of diplomacy, which is a different mode of engaging the world than criticism. And that the idea of criticism as a way to differentiate the world in the pursuit of goodness, as *discrimination* again, has generated a medusa's head of problems. Here's one: if you've made up your mind to like everything beforehand is that not prejudice? Prejudice again! And can you have a prejudice against discrimination? It's another question for Katrina.

9

Life and Art

Later that afternoon she and I are sitting in her shining house out in IJburg, the new town built on reclaimed land on the edge of the city. The place is clean and slick and rectilinear, and compared to my rickety old galleon of a place in tourist Amsterdam, which is all character and billowing sails stitched up with twine, Katrina's house seems to me like one of those hi-teck Sunseeker power boats with a spectral paint-job and a diving deck at the stern. I keep that to myself – it's another boat analogy – and sip my coffee and concentrate on the subject at hand. Prejudice and discrimination. But in Katrina's hands, the subject turns to life and art. She ridicules a contemporary artist who said he wanted to *get away from that whole proscenium arch thing*, and then took hold of the glass of water on the lectern in front of him and held it up, so it glinted in the light like a malevolent charm.

A work of art is an idea, he said. *A concept. If I say this is a work of art that's what it is.*

"Do you see what happened?" says Katrina. "The art object has just been reduced to a representation of an idea; but, since the glass of water is itself a piece of the world, a piece of life, it has been reduced to a representation of itself! That's a double proscenium arch!" Pop! It's enough to make you jump out of your pan!

You can ask the question *what is art?* and just about get away with it but ask the question *what is life?* and everyone thinks you're making a joke. That doesn't stop people asking what they should do any more than it stops them asking what they should like. In the days of tradition, everyone knew their place and what they had to do. The great confusion of now, says Katrina, is that the pecking order is not explicit, but it's still very much intact.

She jumps up and searches the bookshelf for her copy of Morton Feldman's book *Give my Regards to Eighth Street*, which is a collection of miscellaneous writings that add together to a memoir of life in the New York art colony of the middle nineteen fifties, in the formative pre-post-modern days. The days of Jackson Pollok's unpremeditated paintings, and John Cage's music of Zen silences. Feldman himself was a composer, and has a lot to say about music, and a lot to say about painting. And about being an artist; all with the understanding, it seems, that there is knowledge, and there is what you know; that you need to believe in nothing and to live in the present.

"Listen!" She says. She reads out a bit about Cage gradually talking less and less about the Zen as his work develops. "*At most he would give it a sort of warm pat on the shoulder, like some old friend he was leaving in a comfortable bar in Tokyo while he himself began his trek across the Gobi Desert.* Great, huh?" She says. "'His trek across the Gobi desert!'" She goes on. "That's the struggle of making art. And somewhere here there's another bit about that, and how it became stranger as they got to the end of this time he's talking about, what does he say?" She flips the pages, searching, "here we are: *what was great about the fifties is that for one brief moment nobody understood art. It lasted maybe six weeks.*" She laughs: "Maybe for six weeks!" She says, "imagine! When artists escaped art history, when they weren't celebrities, when they were anonymous – and that's actually how they wanted to be! Imagine that feeling, everybody defining art by doing it, no one trying to forecast what their reception was going to be."

Or what art *means*, or what it's *for*.

"And here's something for you." She starts reading again. "Now, almost twenty years later, I ask myself why everybody knows so much about art. Thousands of people – teachers, students, collectors, critics – everybody knows everything." She flourishes her hand in the air. "Here it is, now listen: *To me it seems as though the artist is fighting a heavy sea in a rowboat, while alongside him a pleasure liner takes all these people to the same place."* I guess he's talking about the criticism industry. She snaps the book shut and holds it up like the torch of knowledge. "I love this book," she says.

I tell her an art-spat story I once heard about the Farnsworth House in Chicago, USA. It's a house all made of glass, showcasing the chic austerity of the great modern architect Mies van der Rohe. It was built beside the river Fox on a plot that was then open country but is now swallowed up by the low-rent suburbs of the city. The new owner of the house – an art patron, who else would buy such a place? – commissioned the sculptor Andy Goldsworthy to make a piece for the garden. The artist is famous for his in-wilderness constructions of in-locality materials. He took pieces of stone from the riverbed and arranged them into an art piece; but soon afterwards a gang of South Chicago boys broke into the plot and, finding this pile of stones, hurled them all back into the river they came from! Bump, thump, laugh!

I don't even know if this story is true, but it starts me thinking of the survival of artworks and whether their only real value is what the philistines call *standing the test of time*. If it's been here a while, if no one's had the guts to recycle it yet, like Chartres Cathedral, say, or the Mona Lisa, then it must be good: but what about that Head Made of Frozen Blood, living its precarious life like a stone Buddha in Taleban country, festooned with post-it notes to the cleaners not to unplug the refrigeration? What if it's not a work of art at all, but a piece of criticism? I'm suggesting that because the story is bigger than the work itself. What about that Pile of Bricks in store in the basement stacked up, so help us, like a pile of bricks? Is it art? And what about the Unmade Bed! Is that art, too? Or is it a set of iconic linens like the shirt worn by Horatio Nelson at the battle of Trafalgar, the one in the Maritime Museum, the one with the bullet hole in it from the bullet that killed him? Iconic linens doomed to a future of high value, pored across by conservators with tweezers removing specks of dust from the weave of threads one by one. I can feel the horror of the chambermaids. Do not disturb? Why the hell not! They could wash the sheets. They could *make the bed* – they could solve the problem of art just like that. They could solve art, with life!

I can feel myself becoming wolf. I tip my own head back and point my own grey snout at the sky to howl my own howl – but at this moment, Katrina's little boy Jacob skids into the room clutching a doll made of modelling clay. It looks grotesque, a hunchbacked voodoo mannequin ready for torture. "Papa!" he says. "Look at Papa!" He pirouettes towards a chest in the corner and pulls the drawers open one by one until he finds what he's looking for and pulls out another doll, this time an elaborate construction made of cardboard and sticky tape. "Mama!" he yells. He mashes them together. Then he points straight at me and says "I'll make one of you!" and runs out of the room.

"Hey Mister Freud, let it go!" says Katrina to my startled face. "He's a kid! He's playing!"

I HAVE A BOOK IN MY STUDIO called *The Aesthetic Theories of French Artists*, by Charles Edward Gauss. It is about the influence of science on painting. Charles Edward Gauss is not like Katrina's choice Morton Feldman, the up-from-the-streets expressionist. He is an East Coast academic, writing just after the Second World War and just before the beat generation of pre-postmodernists got going. He could be one of those guys on the pleasure liner that Feldman was writing about. In the stuffy language of his time he says things in his introduction like this: *In rendering the French quotations in English I have made my own translations, though often better ones are available, in order that any responsibility for misunderstanding may be laid only to me.* Thus neatly playing the academic's trick of being humble – a poor thing but mine own – and showing off – I can translate French – at the same time. I'm sure Gauss was a decent man, but I was once attacked by one such closet egoist who was not: in a book launch seminar, my words traduced, my published views labelled racist, militarist and sexist, even as I was sitting there next to him – and as I blurted out my defences, blood gushing from every wound, he said, "I'm sorry. Didn't know you'd take it so hard. Still – as Nietzsche said, what doesn't kill you makes you stronger." This said with a smile. Hand stretched out for a shake. Which I refused. *The difference between you and Nietzsche,* I managed to get out, between gasps of rage, *is that when Nietzsche said that, he was using his own words.* And I've thought since that maybe it's guys like him who are the wolves in the Little Red Cape story.

Aesthetic Theories of the French Artists is an account of the coming into being of modern painting from Courbet's realism via impressionism and post-impressionism and cubism to surrealism. It traces in straightforward terms the impact on art of the arc of scientific revelations about the hidden nature of the material world. For example particle theory: photons streaming from the sun and bouncing off things and striking the retina is what the impressions of Impressionism are. And 'Mr. Freud's' theories of the unconscious are what surrealism is. After the high-density tomes spewing out of today's academies, it is refreshing: Impressionism is a depiction of the photons striking the retina. Surrealism is a depiction of the psyche. Modern art is all about science. So could we add that conceptual art is an imitation of quantum physics and its conundrums about the role of the observer? It all sounds plausible - but then, if it's life and art it could all be just kids' stuff. Maybe all art angst is kid's stuff. Phenomenology, for example: *if I shut my eyes does the world cease to exist?*

"Hey, Fronk!" Katrina says. Fronk staggers into the room fully laden with a projector slung over his shoulder, projector stand in one hand, computer in the other, plugs and leads trailing behind him with a clatter and a sheaf of papers perilously tucked under his arm. "Did you forget the chairs or something, Fronk? We've got thirty people coming tomorrow."

10

The Globeskin

In the event, it's more like a hundred. We are out on the edge here. The new town of IJburg is being built on an artificial island made of sand dredged from the seabed just outside the city. It's an inhabited building site. Every so often the grid of roads stops abruptly at a wire fence, behind which the ground is churned up by underground works and the tracks of yellow diggers and blue and green cement trucks. There's sand everywhere. It's like a frontier town in a western movie. But they've got the tramlines in, and the cycle tracks are all linked up with the city so it's already a suburb of Amsterdam and so suffers from anti-suburb snobbery. But it also slots in to the Dutch tradition of making new land, of which the first inhabitants are pioneers getting life going from raw beginnings – and another dose of snobbery, this time about *polderfolk,* provincial turnip heads, is heaped on the IJburgers. The double dose induces a community spirit as tough as that soccer crowd. All Fronk has to do is stick a notice in the supermarket window about this lecture he's giving entitled *GLOBESKIN,* and he gets a full house.

There are too many for indoors, so we set up in the little square outside, and sit there wrapped in scarves and coats against the cold under a sky blooming with the yellow glow of Amsterdam to the west and sprinkled with stars on blackness to the east. Fronk sets a series of images to play brightly on a screen that gently oscillates in the breeze; images of life lived in nature, not alongside it. In the actual world, not the real one.

The Globeskin of the title is a map drawn on a buffalo skin by plains Indians in North America just before the civil war. The map shows a battle between different tribes, with pictograms of men on horses wearing headdresses of feathers and wielding axes and guns. Fronk tells us that the North American aboriginals of the great plain, those wild-west show Indians with their horses and guns swooping down on circles of covered wagons full of palefaces, were a recent phenomenon. Until the curse of seventeenth century Europe arrived, slashing and burning and clearing and building, native Americans lived close to actuality in cheerful communities that only took a couple of hours a day to gather what they needed to survive and spent the rest of the time partying, singing, dancing and making love. And sometimes, a little bit of war. Fronk makes it sound like student life on the barricades in Paris in nineteen sixty eight. He shows us a picture of a Powhatan party in Delaware painted in 1603 by one of the Early English settlers, John Smith. The aboriginals are dancing in a circle, dressed in branches and fronds, round three naked girls who stand with their limbs intertwined exactly like the three graces in the Hellenistic statue now in the Louvre – *did he draw what he saw or what he knew?* Asks Fronk. It was the time of the renaissance, after all.

All around, the faces of the audience are lit up by the picture on the screen, their brains churning with the thoughts Fronk is knocking out, a party made not of singing and dancing but of information transmission. I steal a glance at Katrina with Jacob on her lap. She looks like a marble Madonna, until she turns her head and smiles and animates the vision. It grabs my heart. Love is another word for unfinished business, I think. Jacob stares at me from his perch on her lap like a baby owl, and I turn my attention back to the screen.

The aboriginals of the American forest were knocked westwards by the European invasion and moved out onto the plains, says Fronk, where they took up Spanish horses and English guns and became nomadic, following the buffalo herds and living off their meat, and using their skins for clothes and shelter and for drawing maps like the Globeskin, which is the next image.

"I call it the Globeskin because it is a picture of everything," he says. "Life and death, community, territory, all gathered into the present moment." He draws our attention to a strange pattern in the top right corner of the battle, a sort of roundel made of dark dots with a red blotchy mass at its centre. "I want to show you what art can be, when it is also close to nature, when it is of the present moment," he says, and throws up a larger detail of it on the screen. The red blotch turns out to be the headless body of a horse, stuck all over with spears, which bristle like the spines of a broom. The head of the horse, and also the heads of five scalped human beings, are arranged in a circle round the bloody torso, the human faces with expressions of horror, mouths open, eyes open, staring at the sky. The dark dots of the roundel turn out to be the impressions of hooves, presumably where the makers of this gruesome battlefield trophy have galloped round and round it to make a sort of mandala in the sandy ground. Fronk calls it *the art of the present moment!*

The next picture, suddenly completely different, is a photograph of the blue sky above IJburg, taken that morning, an image fresh as wild flowers – and the sky is laced all over with contrails. The same contrails that I saw this morning setting off for school with Trogo. But for Fronk, contrails carry the same sort of present moment significance as the battlefield trophy does. They are the traces of violent action, the noisy fury of jet combustion, taken in pursuit of human desire. *They preach zero carbon and then plunge into debt at the first sign of trouble,* says Fronk! *Paying it back will keep us carbon heavy for another twenty years!* Big cheer. Katrina turns and smiles at me again. Because now we have an IJburger debate on our hands. It is on the pressing subject of our time, climate change. And: *what the fuck can we do about it?* Or, as the IJburgers say, *wat de fuck gaan we doen?*

AN OLD GUY WITH A GREY BEARD gets slowly to his feet and announces that he has an answer to climate change. With his red silk cravat and mustard yellow cords and his blue blazer he looks like an old school roué. He says it is a three-step program, and will cost nothing. The preamble is delivered in full Dutch grandfather style, full of gentle humour and a heavily implied expertise in making love.

"Don't tell me about present moments, Fronk, I've accumulated more of them than you," he says. He rubs his hand across his head. "But you know, all you lovely girls," – he is older than every woman in the room – "there is only one present moment. Life is made of it."

When he finally gets to the point, it is tough love. Global warming is inevitable. If human made, it is too late to stop. If it's another spin of the cycle that produces the ice ages, whatever that is, then it's too big to stop. Sea levels are rising and the climate is changing. We can measure it and feel it already. So why waste time on trying to stop the world changing when we could be inventing ways to live with the change? "After all" he says, "and you all know this – the world is always changing."

He imagines life restabilising after global warming has transformed the world. When the humans are pitched into a second dark age, a life no longer illuminated by television screens. We will want less. We'll have less. There will be no work as we know it, but there will be plenty of digging to do. "And the Dutch know how to dig, am I right?" He says. We will dig to raise the dikes against the sea but also we will dig to make defences against the swarms of nomads who will be released when the bonds of civilisation snap. "So step one: we stay where we are and we dig ditches."

Everyone there can imagine this. Every Dutch school kid knows the pictures of the work camps building the polders after the Hitler war. Muddy boots, striped pyjamas, tin cups. But then he says: "step one, the ditches. Step two, we start to build cathedrals again." And how can we do that? How can we set about building another Chartres when we're starting from scratch?

"The cathedrals were built with cash," he says. "Built one piece at a time." When the money was gone, he says, they would stop for a few years, maybe for a generation, until they could afford another doorway, another couple of bays. "That's why they took two hundred years to build, and that's why they are so fine; they are an accumulation of present moments. They are *old guys*." He twinkles fiercely. "The buildings made today are so highly leveraged and value engineered and paid for with debt that they are rushed into being to earn their living. That's why they look like kitchen cupboards!" Fronk starts clapping, so do the rest of them. That's it: after the global warming, we want less because we have less. We spend our time digging ditches, and slowly erecting, piece by piece, the new cathedrals.

Someone shouts out: *and where do we live?*

"That's step three. We live like poor people always live. We use what comes to hand."

"Look at this," says Fronk. He punches a key on his computer and brings up a picture of a place entirely made out of recycled materials. An African township. All cheek by jowl and open sewers in the red sand of the streets. Corrugated iron and plywood walls, plastic sheet roofs held down with car tyres and rocks, territories marked out with crowd control barriers yanked from the contested streets of Johannesburg, washing lines strung with old blankets of all sizes and colours, the longstanding fruits of western charity. If you try you can see the mirage of the cathedral hanging over this heap of jumble as light as a cloud. "Soweto," says Fronk, and the old guy practically bursts into tears.

"It's beautiful," he says. "All that and sunshine too!"

AT THE AFTER PARTY it seems like the whole population of the island is jostling for space. There's a big bonfire burning, and a table of things to eat, and a long crowded bar table already sodden with spills, and a band playing. Four women hitting their guitars like they hated them. The band is called *Morning Wood*. I stand and watch, mesmerized by the beauty and aggression of the lead singer.

"Don't even think about it," says a voice beside me.

"Huh?"

"That's my girl," he says. He's American. "You know what Morning Wood is, huh?" Looks at me with a leer. "That's my girl," he says again. And even at this distance you can feel the heat. Legs like a horse. Arse like a pear. Lithe as a snake. "And is she bright?" He says. "Is she bright? Ask her anything you like, man, she'll tell ya!"

Suddenly I see a familiar face on the other side of the bonfire.

"Do you know who that is?" I ask him.

"Well he looks like the guy Katrina's been hanging out with. The pimp. But that's not him."

"He's a pimp? Know that for sure?"

"Well, he looks like a pimp and quacks like a pimp, take a wild guess, man."

At that moment Katrina comes up and grabs my arm and leads me across the grass like a woman leading a horse.

"He just told me that Bamba's a pimp!" I blurt out, and she laughs.

"Here! This is Bob. Paul, Bob. Bob, Paul," she says and I find I'm standing in front of the climate change grandfather. "Bob has something to tell you," she says, and then disappears back into the crowd. The cold night is lit up by the flames of the fire and the cacophony of Morning Wood mixes with the warmth of the mulled wine.

"Beautiful creature," says Bob, looking after her. "I'll miss her when I'm gone." He looks at me with his eyebrows raised. Where is he going? "I'll miss myself when I'm gone," he says. "In fact I miss parts of myself already!" He laughs and grabs my elbow and switches on a little burst of charm, which is so persuasive that I tell him I liked what he said, liked the cathedral thing, liked the Soweto thing as well, in fact liked the ditch thing! I said I liked it all. It's not some back-to-green-nature sustainability fantasy, it's fully metropolitan, I gushed. I couldn't stop myself.

"Katrina told me about your *Everything* project," he says. "I've got something for you." And he started to describe the early days of planet Earth, when the gravitational collection of space rocks had formed the sphere, and the heat and brimstone of collision and volcanic eruption had settled down, and the resultant atmosphere was made of carbon dioxide and nitrogen – the only oxygen on Earth was tied up as CO_2 with Carbon molecules in the air and as H_2O with Hydrogen molecules in the waters of the oceans, waters that had condensed out of the steam of the volcanoes.

"What happened next," says Bob, staging his words with his craggy old hands while I look on, dumb as a puppy, "was that bacteria evolved to live in the oceans and started to photosynthesize the carbon dioxide and freed oxygen into the atmosphere. You know how big a billion is? In your life your heart beats two and a half billion times," he says, thumping me softly in the chest with his fist. "And that's how many *years* it took, two and a half billion, but gradually they built up reservoirs of free oxygen in the atmosphere, like oases in the desert, until at last they coalesced and there was enough for oxygen breathing animals to start evolving." Thumps me again, a little harder this time. "We evolved into a created world!" is his point. "You and I, all of us, we evolved alright, but the atmosphere that made it possible was created!"

It's a creation evolution reconciliation. The world was not created by god, but it was created. By another life form: follows function follows form follows function follows form.

Katrina slides up and puts one arm through Bob's. "Two of my favourite guys in the same place at the same time!" she says.

And there is so much more to say I am stunned to silence. What you can see on the horizon is the spatial equivalent of the accumulation of present moments. Walk, and keep walking, and the horizon changes as life is lived. That kind of thing. And I don't want to feel Katrina's ridicule at this moment in time.

"This old guy's kind of cute, don't you think?" she says, and gives Bob a kiss. And as I'm trying to frame an answer to this impossible question along comes little Jacob. Way past his bedtime, pushing through the throng of adults like a guppy on the seabed, eating an ice cream cone. He is taking little bites of it and spitting them on the floor. Which is a completely original way to eat an ice cream cone, and an artwork of the present moment if ever I saw one. And sticking out of his pocket is another: a cardboard and sticky tape doll; a little Bob doll.

The Only Possible World

In Voltaire's 1759 satire 'Candide', he lampoons the philosopher Dr. Pangloss for the positive spin being peddled. Pan-gloss means explain-everything. To every fresh disaster that befalls his innocent – ignorant? – young friend Candide, he reasons that 'everything is for the best in the best of all possible worlds.'

Dr. Pangloss is a parody of the German philosopher Leibnitz, who was one of the three great seventeenth century rationalists, with Descartes and Spinoza. They all shared the same difficulty; they had to reconcile reason with the creation. It is of consequence for us that the age of reason was constructed before Darwin, and that we have had to adapt it to our needs – a mass of confusion has flowed from the patching up that that has entailed. But in those days it was too dangerous to publicly describe a world that had not been made by god. For Descartes, the division between mind and matter could be reconciled by divine dispensation. For Spinoza, nature itself was synonymous with divinity. And Leibnitz said that everything that existed did so independently of everything else, but in a set of relations chosen by god – this world is the best of all possible worlds because god has selected it out of the infinite choice he had. How much plainer would reason be if it kicked divinity out! For example – this is the best of all possible worlds because it exists in the present. There is, actually, in the second it takes you to read this sentence, no other way for it to be. This is the only possible world.

All the time in this book I have been making a distinction between the real world and the actual world. The real world is the matrix that frames our lives. It is not one world; it is whatever we imagine it to be, whatever we agree, by custom or force, to say it is. Money, politics, technology and faith are what frame it. War and justice are its life and death matters. At any time on the globe, there are many such worlds. They change slowly as the generations devolve and empires rise and fall. They are complex, but understandable.

The actual world is the thing itself. Unlike the real, it is simple but incomprehensible. It is the spinning planet and everything on it as it is *now, in the present, in this split second. It is not the same thing as it was ten minutes ago, or ten years ago, or ten million years ago. That turbulence is what the real worlds are trying to arrest with their histories and their plans; but in the actual world, there is no past and no future, only the present. All we know of it is in the present. All we know of the past we know because it is here with us now, in living memories or in the material record, whether books, pictures and buildings, or fossils and sediments. The Parthenon, the greatest building in the world, is of the past, but stands here in the present, in ruins, on its sacred hill. The perfection we know it had is gone, now only described in the chronicles; but we know about it because those chronicles too are with us in the present. And the future? What we know of the future, all the plans we lay, all the projections we make, are here with us too, hatching in the present.*

The present matters to How To Like Everything because the idea of everything, with its preposterous inclusiveness, is only manageable in that way. In the instant, we can say, there is everything: but the next instant will produce its own new catalogue. When I carried this suggestion into a seminar at the art school they all objected. The serial instants of the incoming present – next, click, next, click, next – are too short to carry any information. There must be some duration for 'everything' to show itself – and how long is that? A camera can freeze a galloping horse at a thousandth of a second. A blink of your eyes is one twentieth. Both so short you don't notice them. So how long is the present in which everything shows itself?

Try this. Why are hit singles three minutes long? Is it the short attention span of contemporary youth? Or is that the length of time it takes to perceive something new. Think of yourself looking at something for the first time, how long did it take to sink in? Is that it? Is the present three minutes long? Maybe it's three days. Or the Jesuit's seven years! Give me the boy for seven years and I will show you the man. Or perhaps it is your whole life – because the riposte to the assertion of 'no past, no future, only present' is the duration of a human life, with all its accumulated memories. It is the overlapping of generational memories that produces a consensus – inside the tribe – about the nature of the world.

Go on, call me a post modernist. Jackie's psychotherapist does. I would prefer the term post structuralist, in fact to split a hair, I would prefer to be called a speculative actualist, but she doesn't care. She says people like me, in trying to escape the structures of society, are leaping into a lonely void. "What?!" I insist: "people like me? There is no one like me!" – meaning, there is no typical human. And she says, there you have it, there's your problem right there. We can agree on nothing. She looks hard at her damaged patients and pieces together her theory of what it is to be human. She can do without God because old-school structuralists like her are humanists. They describe the world's relations as human constructs, and uncover human absolutes in their studies of different cultures, which they say are the archetypes and principles for right living. Post structuralists, in contradiction, say that substituting human for god is not enough. There is no right way of living. Being human is a temporary state. All worldly relationships are dynamic and there is no value that can be described as absolute.

"Is that so?" She says. "Are you telling me there's no truth? Okay! Then I won't believe you!"

Modernist humanists like her don't need names, they don't need personalities, they need the truth. Post modernism, by contrast, is a quagmire of cross-reference and attribution. Its materialism needs the bodies, so it's person-dependent. The Hells Angels were originally fighter pilots, returned from the war in Germany all hopped up with the adrenalin of fighting and killing and unable to settle back into ordinary life. You could start Post modernism with them. You go on with the beats, Kerouk and Ginsberg and Ferlinghetti with their experimental howling, you continue with Debord and COBRA and the Situationists and the society of the spectacle and abstract expression and student protest – is that all kid's stuff? Then on with Foucault and Deleuze, hammers in hands and the sparks flying; and with Derrida and Lyotard who encapsulated the impulse and put it into slogans that everyone could understand. Deconstruction! The postmodern sublime!

What have these people done? Their intention may have been to slow the supertanker of the Western modern project in its progress, to tug it to a stop – but what if the new project itself is just another description of change, another bloody metaphorical boat? Rather than being another radicalism, another swing of the pendulum, the promise of the post modern is not to recast change but to reframe the understanding of it. In order that we may ask, what is civilisation? It may not be for progress. It may not be for defending the perimeter. It may not even be for equality.

"Right," says the psychotherapist. "Hence the mess we're in."

4
Philosophies

and maybe i'm such a poor avant-gardist because i'm mainly concerned with the present which if i can find it might let me know what to do and as for the future it will find us all by itself
David Antin, *what it means to be avant-garde*

11

Context

If you take a winter transatlantic flight from Europe to the central USA, from Amsterdam to Chicago, there comes a moment about halfway when the great circle route takes you over the coast of Greenland. On a cloudless day, after you've spent hours staring at the grey green North Atlantic five miles below, the coast of Greenland appears suddenly, a mass of gunmetal grey rocks littered with snow and rimmed by bright turquoise icebergs. It's as pretty as the magic kingdom. And if the flight's been steady up till then, with nothing but the background hum and the rustle of newspapers to keep you awake, this is where the heavy jet will start to rock and quiver in the clear air turbulence of the jet-stream, the huge wings flexing, the engine nacelles oscillating, reminding you of the breathtaking actuality of doing what you're doing. It's a great moment. One of those moments when you remember that you're not an automaton with a mortgaged future and a signed-for place in the pecking order – you're a self.

I wish I could rock you like that. Give you a tremor of significance. But a book is not a death defying punt at a distant objective, a book is a book is a book is a book. And what is that exactly? How the big jet stays in the air can be explained with a little trust on your part about the physics of combustion and aerodynamic vacuums, but how does a book do what it does? How does a writer write about everything, when everything is so big?

It may be that not every writer is trying to write about everything – just trying to describe bits of it. Sex in the city. The decline and fall of the Roman Empire. But my suggestion is that all writers, whether trying to or not, are writing about everything, because the context of everything is, in the end, what meaning is.

It's impossible to do because that 'everything' is a complexity at the same time obvious and elusive, simultaneously as plain as the nose on your face and as mysterious as the bottom of the ocean. Miraculous is not too big a word for it – and because it's impossible to write about everything, we write about parts of it instead. We choose which parts to write about and we juxtapose them in the hope that the sparks arising from the collisions with the fragments in the reader's head will add up to more than the sum of the parts and an image of everything – yes, in some cases clearer than in others – rises off the page.

A narrative is the selection a writer makes out of everything that there is in the world. Take the story of Little Red Cape, in which she makes her way through the forest to her grandmother's house. The forest is an image of the whole wide world of everything, and the narrative is a path picked out of that world, a selection of elements that matter to the story. The instruction not to dally, the flowers she dallies to pick, the wolf she meets, the state of her grandmother's eyes, ears and teeth, the come-a-little-closer my dear, the swallowing, the woodman with his axe bursting through the door, the rush of guts as the wolf's belly is sliced open and the girl is pulled out by her ankles all slick like a new born. The writer selects pieces out of the everything that there is to describe, and that's the narrative; and together those pieces make a context, the basket in which the elements of the story coexist, in relationships that give them meaning. A context is a set of relationships with meaning. Writers use narratives to select from everything there is, and make contexts by putting the pieces into relation; that's what writers do, they make contexts. The complication – the miracle – is that everything in the world is already in context by definition, you are putting it into context by your attempts to understand it, maybe even by your simple existence; and what the writers are trying to do is help to bring it into perception. The 'plastic' artists who are not writing but making things – and this includes Fronk

the architect, carefully placing his bricks on top of each other –
are not making contexts, they are making pieces of the world
itself. They do it by rearranging the material of the world in a
different form and putting it into place, and leaving it to you to
give it context. What are you going to do? Hate it or like it?

THAT'S THE CORE OF A LECTURE I'M GIVING, on narrative
and context. I've left Lola and Jackie behind in Amsterdam and
I'm rushing to Chicago and back on a two day trip. The lecture to
be delivered in full jet-lag mode in what will feel like the middle
of the night. And now the big plane is on final approach. The kid
in the seat next to me on the United Airlines 777, Amsterdam to
Chicago, flight UA6007, is listening in to the air traffic control
banter on one of those plane spotter radios.

United heavy six double oh seven, says a woman's voice. *United
heavy, go around one more time flight level two zero I have Air America
incoming then North West then you.*

*Okay Suzy, united heavy six double oh seven one circuit two zero
keep me posted.*

The informality of the language sounds like a dress code. Like
smart-casual. The view out of the airplane window is no longer
the distant ocean or the ice covered tundra of Northern Canada
but the big blue of Lake Michigan with the tall buildings of
Chicago fringing it, and then the wing dips low into the final turn
and the *cabin crew prepare for landing* message bongs on and the
wingtip slides over the lakeside towers and then over the huge
expanse of the suburban city beyond, dropping into O'Hare over
the lines of cars and trucks on the freeway, which look from up
here like toys, silently imitating life.

I say goodbye to the kid with the radio and wish him well.
He's just joined the Fire Service of Green Bay, Wisconsin, he says.
One hundred and fifty miles north on the same lake. He's sixteen
years old and looking forward to a life of public service. At the
line later on I can see he's getting on well with the immigration

guys. They can tell he's one of them. He speaks the brotherhood of the uniform. Unlike me. When it's my turn the woman at the counter looks friendly, straight as a die, but a little bit of long term civil service exhaustion clings to her, plus a little aura made of the power of her position. She's like a very polite guard dog. Who are you? She says with her eyes. And then: that's what you say – but can you prove it? I hand over my passport. I am not an automaton with a signed up place in the pecking order, I am a self. An individual. A contextualising force. But to pass through the security gates you need identity, not individuality. They are not the same thing, though the two words get used to mean the same thing. Identity is a question of being identical, the same as the others in your tribe: identifiable. It's the uniform that others put upon you. Individuality is a question of being unique: indivisible. Though your passport invades your person to locate you in the tribe, by fingerprint, by retinal scan, by measure, you need nothing but yourself to be an individual. You don't even need your name. Especially not your name.

There have been times working on this project when I've been aware that liking everything might depend on maintaining that complex but anonymous state of selfhood. Where is the community, the humanity and the society in the idea? What use is it? Know what you know – believe in nothing – live in the present: they're all slogans of the individual over the collective.

If you deep-google *how to like everything*, you will bring to light an article written by John Betjeman, the poet, the Juvenal of twentieth century middle class England, and the first young fogey in the history of the term. An old fogey is a crusty, conservative dinosaur in tweeds and a gold rimmed monocle and a paisley cravat; a young fogey wears the same clothes but is a radical. A mid-century neo-con. In nineteen fifty seven Betjeman and his friends made a move against the by then fully established modernism, and their *how to like everything* was a controversial appeal on behalf of Victorian architecture. Up until that point it had been reviled by everyone for its fussy bourgeois arrangements and its hierarchical set-up; but, according to this new description, it was an architecture of human scale and detail, adaptable, useful and interesting. They could have stopped there – their pitch was an early post modernism, it could have said *how to like this as well as that*. 'Post' could have meant 'after' and not 'instead of'. But the dialectical habit of our age is too powerful. They became opposition merchants just like the modernists they railed against. They waved their hands at brutal town centre developments made of filthy grey concrete, dank harbours of anti social behaviour, and declared the self evident horror of the modern project. They were by and large successful in their crusade, and a revisionary historicism started to replace those horrors. Which was so horrific in its turn that another generation now has to shake its fists all over again at the results. At the little pitched-roof toy-town estates, the gratuitous ornament and the sycophantic traditionalism. The debate goes on, the ping and the pong, the never ending how to hate everything that went before, perpetually turning over the ground and leaving behind nothing but a muddy morass, like a pig-rooted field.

Humanity? Community? Society? What are they, but rationalizations of the pecking order? Of violence made verbal? And democracy – does that ever exist, or are we just dazzled by the possibility of consensus right in the midst of our unsolvable differences? Look at the idea of it. It's a majority thing. It's not about freedom, it's about conformity. An issue comes up, we vote on it, and what the majority wants, happens. The idea is that the outvoted ones then conform – they accept the decision. Not to retire and lick their wounds and fight again another day, but to take the majority view to heart, and get on with it with good will. But how often does that happen?

THE TRAIN FROM THE AIRPORT into the city of Chicago rattles along on its elevated rails passing through mile after mile of dilapidated buildings from the old days, brick upon brick by the million, fire escapes of rusting iron, roofs patched with black tar, rotting wood windows and everything covered in grafitti. Squalor as only rich America can do it, I reflect like an old fogey. But now suddenly here's the fireman kid from the airplane!

"Excuse me sir, is that seat free?" I shuffle up my stuff and he sits down, but he looks as alert as a hawk, ready to spring up again any second.

"I decided to get a later train to Green Bay. I had to get in and see the city. I really, really like this grafitti," he says. "And all this old stuff, it's so cool. You know where the best grafitti is? Berlin."

"You never been to Brooklyn?"

"No, sir! Been to New York but I didn't get out of Manhattan. One long party that was, I can tell you." He switches on his teen bravado and starts to describe the party and I begin to regret letting him sit there but then he catches a glimpse of an impossible to reach tag high up on a bridge and his enthusiasm slips him back into the present. Back into himself. "It was awesome to be in Amsterdam after New York. You know New York used to be New Amsterdam? Used to be Dutch? You know when they got there they decided to make it a model of old Amsterdam? You know that big street that runs through the centre, the Damrak?"

He's got me nodding like a dashboard dog with all his questions. Yes, I know the Damrak. It's a street now, but at the time of New Amsterdam it was the big wide central canal. "See they made Broadway to be like that," he goes on, "a wide thoroughfare down the middle of the new city and the Battery, where the fort was, that's like the Dam itself." The Dam is the original lump of clay and sand that Amsterdam is founded on. "There's a curving street, Water Street, in downtown Manhattan, down by the exchange, that's built on the line of a curving creek the settlers found and built up like an Old Amsterdam canal – houses, row houses, along a curving quay with the creek made into a canal to take their boats!"

In other words, New Amsterdam was a direct copy of Old Amsterdam. "You know this for a fact?" I ask him. It's a nice story but how does he know all this?

"It's what my course leader told us. I think it's a fact."

What a great kid. He is the embodiment of a youthful how to like everything. Live in the present – that's his enthusiasm. Know what you know, even if you are the only one who knows it. What else? "What do you believe in?" I ask him.

"Jesus Christ, sir." He says. "Praise the Lord."

Whom I abuse with *believe in nothing*. Praise and abuse! If you can treat those two imposters just the same, I want to say. I don't, because it's something you have to find out for yourself. But he's such an observant kid I want to give him a hint of how to like everything from an older perspective. So I tell him instead about that Thomas Hardy poem where he runs a litany of exquisite private moments out in the natural world. Say it slowly, now: *when, like an eyelid's soundless blink the dewfall-hawk comes crossing the shades to alight upon the wind warped thorn.* And then the poet asks, *Will they say of me one day, "he used to notice such things"?*

"Well, sir," says the sixteen year old kid, shining with life. "I think that *will they say of me* line would be great to have on my gravestone."

12

What, Whow and Wherewhen

Back in Amsterdam again, Lola and I have a rare day together on our own in the house. So we clean it, top to bottom. It feels as intimate as cleaning each other. And while we clean, surrounded by the scent of polish and the soft buff of dusters, we talk. It's lovely, peaceful and domestic. I tell Lola all about old man Bob the artist and what he said about the oxygen of the atmosphere being created, and his three-point plan for global warming. I tell her about the kid on the plane and how he reminded me of the original slogan for this quest of *How To Like Everything* – live in the present, believe in nothing, know what you know. I tell her about the simple but incomprehensible idea that underpins the whole enterprise, which is that there is no past and no future, only the present.

"Oh yes," she says, "your ontology bollocks."

And then she starts telling me about meeting a man on the street the other day who told her about being a Sufi. "You'd like Sufi. They are people of peace. They live in the present – which is to them the present moment in which God's creation continuously unfolds – and because they are located in the present they live without hope but also without fear." It's Islam, Sufi, but it's an Islamism so special, a surrender so deep, it seems not like religion at all. Seems like something else altogether. Lola's right, I do like her description – where Buddhism is about nothing, Sufism is about everything. Buddhism strives for nothing to eliminate suffering, Sufism suffers everything. So I ask her who this Sufi is she's met on the street.

"He's called Bamba. You must have seen him. Drives that big black Audi. Parks it right out there on the bridge sometimes."

"The pimpmobile?" I ask, in horror. "He's a pimp, that guy.

How can he be a Sufi? How can you have a Sufi pimp?"

"He's not a pimp. He runs a charity looking after retired women."

"But I saw him taking money! Right there, outside the house. Big wads of cash."

"That's right," she says, "he runs a charity. He's not a pimp. He helps women. I like him."

Lola sees the best in everyone, but this is ridiculous. So Bamba raises fallen women, I say – to be told that *fallen* is an Old Testament idea. I mean he saves whores from whoredom – no, *saved* is a New Testament idea. Whoring is like any other job, she says. Some people are enslaved by it, some find themselves doing it, some choose to do it, some enjoy it. But they've all got to retire sometime, and Bamba helps them when they do. Is this what they call humanism, or is it something else?

Humanists are structuralists. They believe in structure because they are attempting to reconcile the different ways of being human that have arisen in the world – structure to them is a word for the common features of what it is to be human. So they study language, the prime quality of being human. They catalogue the basic sounds the human pharynx can produce. They invented the universal language of Esperanto in an attempt to bring us all together. They are after unity.

But Lola is not a humanist, she's a vitalist. She believes in structure like humanists do, but she does it on behalf of all life, not just human life. In fact we first met at a seminar in London devoted to a linguistic proposition that was not about unifying humanity with a common language but attempting to make it easier for things like us humans to interface: it was not about Esperanto but about pidgin English. Let me explain.

THIS BOOK HAS BEEN WRITTEN in idiomatic English. It is not the same language as World English, as that Dutchman pointed out back there in public space. In twelve years time people will understand him and not me. Because idiomatic English is dense and rhetorical, full of homely sayings and colonialist assumptions and question marks. Maybe it is untranslatable in the full sense.

English has become the Lingua Franca – an old name for a universal spoken tongue that dates back to the Holy Roman Empire, meaning the language of the Franks – for three reasons. First, Hollywood speaks it. Second, it has ditched most of the details that other languages find necessary – gender and case declension – so it is not so much to learn. Third, it is accidental. At first this seems full of difficult irregularity, but in the end it is an advantage because it makes it resilient – it hardly matters how it is spoken. You can be as clumsy with English as you want. Try speaking Dutch to the Dutch and they will laugh at you because it is rare for them to hear it spoken by a foreigner and they are not used to the distortions in language foreign speakers produce. With English, grammar hardly ever gets in the way of sense. Precision, maybe, but not blunt sense.

The seminar on pidgin English looked at the six questions – who, what, where, when, why and how – to see if the language could be further compressed. The discussion, bizarre as it is, belongs in a book called *How To Like Everything*, because these are the everything questions. They are the questions taught at journalism school, because if you answer them all you know you will have covered your subject. They are called "five w's and an h", which itself is an example of accidental English: why are they not six w's? And what follows is what the seminar concluded.

Who and *what* are about material presence in the world. The difference between them is a species one – who is for humans, what is for everything else. If humans were created beings, that would be a significant difference; but if we are emergent beings, and have evolved through the same processes as everything else, we only need one word. We could combine who and what like this: Whot? That is the epistemological question. *Know what you know.*

Why and *how* are about ends and means. If they could be combined the edifice of moral anxiety that arises out of reasons for action and the methods employed might evaporate. Torture and bombs might not exist! So we could combine why and how like this: whow. Whow? Is the ethical question. *Believe in nothing.*

Lastly, *where* and *when*. One explanation of the present moment, in which the actual world can be glimpsed, is Einstein's theory of relativity. His word 'spacetime' was made to frame the nature of existence. Space is where and time is when, but the two are inseparable; hence 'spacetime'. The two questions where? And when? Could likewise be written together, as 'wherewhen?' So now all questions begin with a w and there are only three of them: Whot, Whow and Wherewhen. Wherewhen is the metaphysical question. It is the question to which the answer is 'herenow'. *Live in the present.*

And here's a complication, pointed out to me after the seminar by Lola on a hilariously romantic bus ride home. If space and time were time and space instead, 'timespace', and the question was not where and when but when and where, 'whenwhere', the answer here and now, 'herenow', would be now and here, which comes together as 'nowhere'. Nowhere! And so, back to utopia. The only possible world.

13

Commitment

The old maps of old Amsterdam are bird's eye views, full of pitched roofs and church spires and merchant ships. Forests of masts line the canals, with a foliage made of rigging and flags. Looking at them you can imagine the noise and bustle of a trading port, with the sky above the quays full of pallets and barrels being hoisted aloft, and the air full of shouts and birdcalls. Now, the big roads on the periphery are full of trucks and the canals of Amsterdam are as quiet as a picture, but there are still plenty of boats. The canals of the centre carry tourist boats, and the old wharves south of the centre are lined with houseboats. The contemporary google's eye view shows them squatting in long lines; flat roofed barge conversions, floating boxes with television aerials instead of masts. Sitting in the water, never moving, they look more static than the buildings on the quayside themselves. Especially on an icy day with the seagulls strutting about on the frozen canal surface.

In one of these boats, down on the Jacob van Lennepkade, lives the old man Bob from the IJburg party. He turns out to be a sculptor and he's invited me to see his work. I tread carefully across the slippery gangplank on to the slippery deck wondering how people who live like this don't just drown. I mean, half a bottle of wine and you're overboard.

"You like sculpture?" He says as soon as I'm inside. The place is all got up in velvet drapes like a sixties fashion photo shoot, but there's no time to take it in.

"Well sure, I ..."

"Look at this." He takes from his pocket what looks like a polished stainless steel washer, but large, maybe 80mm across. It's square, with a hole punched in the centre and it has a twist that makes the hole look peculiarly double sided.

"You put a twist in that simple shape and the hole – that's an absence, right? – suddenly gets two sides when before it had no sides!" He grins. Reaches into his pocket, takes out another. It's the same thing, but this time has another twist that turns the hole into a pouting mouth. He grins again, switches to the other pocket and pulls out a third. "This is what I started with," he says. It's the same washer, but perfectly flat and not polished, still dull, like a metal embryo. "I've been working with this same shape for twenty years now," he says. "I've discovered a whole world in it, just bending it and twisting it. Come and see the piles I have in the back!"

"Wait," I said, but he stopped me.

"I know, you're thinking they're too small, yes? But they have brothers! Big brothers on plinths all over Europe!"

"That's not it." I say. "These are big enough. In fact, they're huge!" I'm thinking that this is exactly what an artist has to do – commit. You strive to like everything but commit to one thing. If everyone likes what you do, great, you'll be a star; if no one does, too bad, but still great, because you've committed.

Contemporary art is talked up as a relational proposition, and so artists are tempted to make art works that have explicit references to other things to place them in the world. It's an attempt to overcome the unity of the object, and place it in its context. But that's not how the world of everything works. "Everything in the world" is in context by definition. The evolutionary, emergent, post modern, whatever it is we're dealing with now view of the world does not require an artist to be multiplicitous – it requires artists to be singular to enable the world to be multiplicitous – in order that multiplicity can sustain. What does mother nature say about that one? A greenfinch is not making reference to the other kinds of finches by its colour; it is committed to the accident of difference in its genes.

But is art accidental? How does accidental genetic transfer

equate to the creation of art? I remember what my art curator friend said about the springtime, when the bushes round her house in rural Scotland were thrumming with the excitement of little birds mating. "It's so wonderful, this time of year. It's when all the genes in the world are reshuffled by sex. When there is a chance for something new to emerge." So is there such a thing as emergent art?

"Hey man, I know where you live," says a voice behind me. I turn around and see the American from that party at IJburg, and right behind him the singer of Morning Wood, whose slender frame seems to fill the doorway. She's basketball tall and lean as a muscle and she looks as implacable as an anaconda. Bob heats up visibly. His cheeks flush and his eyes bulge. He opens a cupboard and pulls out a bottle of genever and glasses and passes them round. Our previous conversation withers like grass in a flame but there's still one more thing I need to know. I sketch out the runes of it for the new arrivals and invite them to pronounce on 'emergent art'. I say that I'm thinking of those computer-aided artists who write algorithms and sit back and let their machines spool out coincidences. The automatic writing. The automatic drawing. What kind of a commitment is that?

"All art is emergent, because everything is," says the anaconda. She seems to rustle when she speaks. "The music of Morning Wood, the music of John Cage *and* the music of Anton Bruckner," she tells me. Just like her boyfriend said she would. *Ask her anything you like, man, she'll tell ya!* "Emergence isn't a mode of operation," she says. "It's an explanation of the workings of the world." She grins loudly, leans in and kisses Bob on the cheeks Dutch style, once, twice, three times and settles back into the velvet.

To make something you have to be committed to it: having made it, you release it into the world and its relationships will accrue. A critic can spend time unravelling or compounding those connections after the event but the artist, using blind chance, makes the things that will be connected. He has to allow the product to emerge from the process. To do that, he has to commit. Sorry, he or she has to commit. Sorry: *IT* has to commit. And that's what you can find to like.

I suppose a *How To Like Everything* survey of artists' commitment could go on forever. The difficult part of setting out to like everything is that all of it, the gently manly struggle of the abstract expressionists, and the hectoring revelations of the surrealists and the prejudiced brilliance of the naive painters, the faith to nature of the pre-Raphaelites and the impressionists and the boss-eyed perception of the cubists, and the enlightenment old masters, and every other nook and cranny, the Venetian school, the New Realists, the Young Brits, see this list will go on forever and I haven't mentioned one actual work yet – or even started on the twenty first century – and the difficult part of liking everything is that all of it, each piece of work, though dependent on the artist's commitment to it and its multiplicity of relations, has equal status. Can you comprehend an equality that big?

THE GENEVER LEVEL slowly travels down the inside of the bottle as the four of us sup it up, and the shadow cast by the low winter sunshine just as slowly moves round the room. We take it in turns to squint in the glare as we talk about sculpture and writing. I explain that I am taking the rash course with *How To Like Everything* by putting it in the first person present. In what other tense should a book about the present be? But no one's going to be able to know what kind of a book it is. Fiction? Memoir? Theory? And then all the fucking happens off stage, and I've filled the thing with characters designed to mouth my thoughts, when everyone tells me that what people are looking for is characters with lives of their own – an illusion of reality. They want to see a conjuring trick.

"Well, what am I?" says the anaconda.

"You're here to help me thrash out left and right. What's that all about?"

She holds up her hands and looks from one to the other. "Left? Right?" She says. She has golden skin on her arms, and golden hairs. I tell her I mean left and right politics.

"For God's sake!" She says. And pitches straight in: "All these this and thats! Context and narrative, creation and criticism, form and function;"

"Form and content?" I add.

"Yes! Form and content! Just another stupid opposition."

As for left and right, she explains: *left wing* is a French revolutionary term for the hard core who gathered together and sat on the left of the general assembly. "It's a seating plan!" She says. The *right wing* is an oppositional formula, developed to describe the opposite sort of hard core. But they're both articulations of the centre, she says. The centre isn't the third way; it's the anchor of the opposition. Left, right and centre are parts of a compound. "If you want to have an alternative to the centre," she goes on, "then don't have a centre. You form a new compound. You don't join the assembly in the first place." This is anarchy, I suppose. A system of peripheries. Those warring baboons come to mind.

"And form and content?" I say.

"Did you hear what I just said?" She says. "Look at you. You are a compound being, a compound of material and ideas, you are yourself content manifested by form. Form animated by content. That's how things exist, as compounds," she says. "And you're writing a book that's all about itself. So what's the form and what's the content? Idiot!"

"You realise I could have you realigned?" I say.

"Oh, go jump in the canal" she yells and clambers to her feet and staggers out of the door. Straight onto the open deck of the houseboat. The next thing we hear is a sharp crack and a muffled splash. She has skidded on the ice and pitched over the side, and is lying there on the surface of the canal cradled in ice shards. Cold and wet but still smouldering. Bob reprimands me for telling a woman like that that she's dispensable, and fetches a long aluminium pole with a shoulder hook on the end and sets about fishing her out. Apparently – I was right – it happens all the time to houseboat people.

BEFORE THEY GO, the American slips me a business card, which has an inscription on the back: *The universe is no narrow thing and the order within it is not constrained by any latitude in its conception to repeat what exists in one part in any other part.* It's from Cormac McCarthy's *Blood Meridian*. It's about everything being different from everything else. The book describes in extremely violent terms the wildness of the Wild West. That wildness is not the wilderness, it is human ambition played out outside the law, unfettered by a common philosophy beyond greed: and consequently the book is deeply moral. Personified in the character of the Judge, who says those words.

Everything in the universe is unique, and the panoply of knowledge we carry in our heads is a grand game of sorting things into piles. Maybe only two piles: *like*, and *don't like*. I want them to stay and discuss it, but the anaconda is still too furious. Which is a shame, because in the end I agree with her. Science and philosophy are both hamstrung by their methods. The dialectics of analytical debate are sidelined by the slow profundity of geologic processes, the settling back into the level ground of every material thing, the uniformitarianism of ultimate existence. But the universe isn't finished yet. It's got five billion years to go with differentiation before we can all lie down flat and like everything in actual terms by becoming everything. That's why the anaconda exploded: the heat of arguments is just another kind of fission, and in plain terms, in species terms, it is so much fun *not* to like everything. Why fight your nature?

Cliff Face Earth

We emerged from the cool darkness of the cave into the dry heat and the bright fierce sunshine of Texas, south central USA. I was there to research the character of empty places in my attempts to build a complete picture of the everything wilderness. The cities are full of everything, easy to see; but how do you see everything where there is nothing? My colleague Saski and I had been on a tour of the Longhorn Caverns in the company of a sadistic tour guide who suddenly snapped off the lantern and plunged us into blackness. He made us count to a hundred before switching it on again.

"Pretty dark down here, huh?" he said. It was – it was total. The caverns snake underground for miles and were once home to a million bats, before the tourist operation arrived. It's so lightless down there it's like being blind, and without the bats' early warning radar, hope turns into fear. The tour guide could have been pulling a Bowie knife from his belt and getting ready to gut us for all we would have known. After all, it was Texas.

Saski and I were taking a break from work and had come out to the middle of nowhere up on the edge of the plateau. We were two hundred miles out of Austin, and it was so quiet and remote there weren't even any planes in the sky. The land for miles around was flat, red sand, dotted with scrubby trees and littered with little rocks like the ones on the surface of Mars. After the caverns we cruised on up to the Buchanan Dam state park. In this part of the world the run off from the sudden storms that whip up in the heat are trapped by dams into turbid reservoir lakes. All the land around is privately owned, except for these water margins, which do double duty as state parks. And it is here, standing on the concrete wall of the dam, that you can look out for miles across the flat landscape and see no one at all.

"This looks just like India," she said. "Where I come from the land is also this flat and the same colour of red. It even has those little black trees."

"Homesick?"

"God, no. If my father found out I'd eaten barbecue, he'd lock me

up!" She smiled with a flash of white. Her hair and eyes are black, her skin's the colour of a chestnut. Face like an arrow. She would look like a native of this place if her expression held less history in it. "You know what's different, though? Here there's no one. Maybe" – she squinted into the distance – "is that a cow? I don't know. In India we would be looking across the land like this and we would see little groups of people, not crowds, just five or six together, maybe with an oxcart, maybe working the land. But we'd look out like this and see little spots of human movement, all over."

The population density varies – India is eleven times more densely populated than the USA – but the landscape is full of people grafting and trading, across the whole surface of the earth. Across the ocean, too. Let us jump space and time together to the Arctic Ocean and the year twenty thirty five: a merchant ship bound from Rotterdam to Yokohama beats North at nought degrees between Kong Frederick the Eighth's land, North Greenland, and Spitzbergen. It is making for the Bering Strait on the other side of the Arctic Ocean, straight over the North Pole. Kong is Norwegian for king; this is an area that has belonged to Norway since the Vikings, but until recently was so seized with pack ice for the whole year round that no one else was interested. Now that the polar pack ice has melted, it is the new short route from Europe to South East Asia, and Norwegian interest has been engulfed by commerce. Trade route opportunities like this have not existed since the discovery of the new world.

This upbeat fantasy in which the catastrophe of the melting pack ice is spun in the other direction, is delivered by an urbane party in a twenty-minute presentation called 'Flat Earth'. He is never more than arm's length from his laptop, on whose screen elaborate parametric diagrams trace possible futures for the human artifice, on this occasion projected across the wall behind him like a psychedelic light show. Perhaps he is practicing for the next TED convention, where alternative mainstreamers, rational optimists the whole bunch of them, gather to discuss Technology, Entertainment and Design. And yet for all his TED-like no problem if we all pull together manner he is spellbinding.

He talks about his polymath hero Buckminster Fuller, who invented the idea of 'Spaceship Earth'. Back in the days of the moon exploration Fuller used to point at the picture of earthrise taken from the surface of the moon, a thing never before seen in the entire being-in-the-world of Homo sapiens, and describe how this simple icon, this image of the fabulously blue and luminous planet all alone in the black vacuum of intergalaxity, ushered in a new understanding of everything. From now on, he said, we shall live in the awareness that what we do to the world we do to each other. We live in a global community of interdependence, on this planet that is a space station, whose safe passage through the future is our responsibility. Spaceship Earth.

Fuller discovered that if he transferred an image of the spherical globe onto a twenty-sided solid and then unfolded the plates onto a flat surface, he could produce a map of the world that did not distort the proportions of the continents. More than that, depending on the way he cut the joins and laid out the plates, the entire landmass of the world from Antarctica to Australia could be represented as one contiguous entity – so making a one-world platform from which to promote the theories of world management that would be needed in piloting Spaceship Earth.

"Look at this," says the urbane party reaching over to his computer, and shows us the dymaxion map, as it was called. "It's like the original single continent, Pangea. The globalized world. Futures traders call it the flat earth, because it has no barriers to trade. I call it the flat earth because inside my computer," patting the machine like a little dog, "there is an algorithm tracing the entire surface, oceans and all, in a single, very long, and need I say flat, set of symbols."

So he has a digital dymaxion map in there! But what does he mean, oceans and all? It is the ocean that negates all flat earth theories, because the ocean has nowhere to go in them: You can see it on the flat earth maps, including Fuller's dymaxion: the ambiguous edge of things where a ship on the perimeter ocean is in danger of sailing straight over the edge and getting lost in space. If the ocean is to be on the earth it must cling to the surface, which implies gravity, which in turn implies a spherical body. In fact the spherical earth was the standard ancient model, a stationary sphere around which the heavens turned and towards the centre of which everything fell. It wasn't until the sixteenth century that Copernicus added spin to the picture: he described the rotation of the earth, which gives us day and night, its tilted axis, that gives us the seasons, and its progress round the sun, that brings the annual solstice festivals. These cosmic dynamics are what give movement to the ocean, and the dispersal of the continents, and the swirling storms and the releasing of the planet's interior energy, the factors that promulgated life itself. Just think of the moon, with the complication of its fertility signature, its twenty eight day cycle, which brings it to the same point above the Earth a little later each twenty four hour day and which drags the ocean tides back and forth a little later each day giving host to a plethora of little sea creatures opening and closing in sync − without the spinning, spherical earth there would be no life and no survival. How could we possibly pilot such a phenomenon?

Meanwhile on a cliff face high above the pounding waves, sea birds nest on tiny ledges safe from predators but with no room to build a nest. Their eggs have evolved towards the conical so when they roll they roll in a circle, and not over the edge and into the sea: the cliff face habitat has bent their lives. And here comes a rock climber, foolhardy, brave, agile, sinew snapping, not on a mission to steal the eggs, but to prove to himself he can climb all the way to the top. He measures his action in spacetime, in space and time simultaneously; exactly where his fingertips and toes have purchase on the minute fissures of rock, exactly how long his twanging muscles can hold the position. Space and time are inseparable in the dynamic world, and just being here, just being alive, is a strenuous activity. He comes face to face with a razorbill on its ledge, which stares at him with its little black eye. The birds on the cliff have no fear of humans. "Spaceship earth?" He yells at it, the sweat of hard work pouring off him: "This is no space ship! We should call it cliff face earth!"

5
Places

"He no longer cared about anything (as before) but now he also cared about everything in principle; that is to say, it was all the same to him and he belonged to the world and there was nothing he could do about it."

Jack Kerouac, *On The Road:* on Dean's final development

14

Aachen

The Inquisition is here again. All three of them texted me at the same time to say they have a car for the day. They're off to Aachen cathedral. They ask me if I want to go to the resting place of King Charlemagne the great, to the one and only *Dom*? Well – does the pope shit in the woods? Of course I want to go. But I can't, I'm looking after Jackie today. *So bring him along!* They say. And in the time it takes me to get the boy ready there is a knocking at the door and the sound of clowning outside. The lanky thin bald one is holding the little one with the big teeth upside down while the dapper one in his slubbed silk suit parades up and down with a hat, pretending to busk money from the tourists.

Come on! They yell. *We're going to Duitsland!* The Dutch pronounce the diphthong 'ui' as a kind of 'ow' with their lips puckered for a kiss. It sounds to my English ears like *doubtsland*. And they all stand to attention and throw their right arms out straight in front of them, but palms upwards, like charismatics at prayer. These guys! I can see today is going to be another lesson in how to like everything by taking nothing seriously. The outlying characters in this book are like the comedians in a sixteenth century comedy. Four comedians for the four humours. *Sanguine*, who speaks with a good heart; *Phlegmatic*, who takes life as it comes; *Colic*, who's angry; and *Melancholic* – who glimpses the terrifying vacuum of the actual world. Bamba is the sanguine, Jackie the phlegmatic, Katrina plus her bubble of Fronk and Jacob are the colic; and these guys, the Inquisition, are the melancholic. Except that the melancholic mode has now trans- formed into the ironic. Speculations on the precarious human condition, including the radical modern's actual world picture of *abyss* and *vertigo* and *schizophrenic* and *delirious*, are now mostly ironic. The Inquisition reduce everything to a common denominator of ironic comic feeds. From the word go: when I run through the circumstance that left me in charge of Jackie today, which was Lola flying out of the house in a sulk as I crawled my way out of my houseboat hangover, The dapper one says to the bald one, "Maybe you shouldn't have told her about him and Katrina!" Giggling. *But why would you do that? There's nothing to tell!* I protest, my heart suddenly thumping with guilt. Cue another outbreak of giggling.

Aachen is clear across the Netherlands past Utrecht and Eindhoven as far as Maastricht, and then a skip across the German border. It's going to take four hours at least, each way. By the time we get back I shall have heard the ironic version of absolutely everything. And why not? Taking nothing seriously is a strategy for survival in this over formalized world. The Inquisition may goof around like teenagers but just because something's kids' stuff doesn't mean it has no value.

In fact these three funny guys have directed me towards a development in what they call *post-postmodern* philosophy: *Speculative Realism*. It is blogged by a bunch of young men like themselves who call the bluff of reason's idealism. There is no necessary link between thinking and being, they say. There is no *I think therefore I am*. There are many things that exist without thinking, from rocks to robots. Maybe even ideas are things, they say. Which puts everything on the same footing and which I interpret as being another route to liking everything. They question rationalism's great tool of the dialectic, and point towards a nature that produces thoughts as it produces mountains or flowers. This possibility brings spirituality, marooned in its ocean of subjective idealism for centuries, back into the material world. And that's what I like about teaching. You sit and tell people about the world and then the world comes back and tells you about itself.

THE CAR IS WHAT THE DUTCH CALL an *old-timer* – it's a thirty-year-old Mercedes coupe with cream leather seats. Very smart but very high mileage and rickety.

"You know, he's a lot like you," says Dapper.

"And he's powered by a propane bomb," says Teeth, showing me the big gas bottle in the trunk, "like a suicide bomber."

There's not much room in a coupe, and Jackie and Bald and I squash in the back astride the transmission tunnel, with Teeth driving and Dapper lounging full length in the front passenger seat. We set off in a profusion of jokes and asides and Jackie's hooting noises and thread out through the old city, then through the not so old city and at last through the downright new, and onto the fast intercity roads that connect us up to the rest of Europe.

As we hurtle south past Utrecht on the dual carriageway we pass all kinds of things in the dense Dutch urbanized version of the landscape. We pass a distribution centre of massive beige warehouses surrounded by razor wire fences and floodlights on tall poles. We see a herd of deer sitting down on the other side of a long dike, with only their antlers visible over the top. We pass forests of white windmills slowly churning time into electricity. We see green sward pastures dotted with cows grazing in between left over patches of snow, which make the ground into an imitation of their own hides. And farmsteads in little willow-bound enclosures looking like postcards. All this landscape tapestry seen at speed, with strings of white and red lights lacing the frosty line of the road before and behind us and a hundred and twenty kilometres an hour beating steadily out of the exhaust. Magnificent. People say that the motorways – freeways, autoroutes – are boring, but it's like everything else. You just have to keep your eyes open.

Jackie won't sit still. He's as interested in what's outside as anybody and wriggles like a squirrel trying to see out of the car. Eventually he clambers clear out of the back across the console between the front seats and, after snagging his pants in the gear shift and plunging us dramatically into neutral, speed flying off the dial and Teeth shrieking like a banshee, he flings himself into Dapper's lap. Vast forty tonne trucks are swinging past us centimetres away and he's behaving like a Skywalker. To the huge delight of the Inquisition, who pick up his squawking hoots like a chorus line as we tear on down the highway.

This circus atmosphere, plus the variety and detail of the journey's sights, gradually evaporates even Dapper's irony, and around halfway, with the high tech smokestacks of Eindhoven slipping past and Jackie restored to the back seat and sleeping like a baby, the entire Inquisition ceases transmission altogether while I sketch out my progress on liking everything to them. Young men, in spite of their talent for speaking in codes, want secrets. They use their ironies like a balloonist uses hot air, to keep the envelope inflated, to keep from crashing into the ground. Deep down they think that knowing the secrets will release them from their perpetual altitude anxiety. I remember one morning at the art school when Bald streamed red-faced and romantic into the studio dressed in a huge army greatcoat whose pockets were full of bottles of beer, clanking like a supply convoy, and threw himself in my face and said, "Tell us the secrets! You know what they are, so tell us!"

Getting older is a question of coming to terms with the fact that you'll never know the secrets; and the resulting equilibrium is what gives the illusion of actually knowing them. So now, every time I think I've stumbled across a glimpse of the actual world, however fleeting, I tell them about it. Today I tell them about the post modern: it was a new view of the same world. Like the theory of evolution, it changed nothing but seemed to change everything by changing the seeing.

Maybe it's not that the world is governed by laws, and that confusions arise from the many ways of looking at the same thing, but, as Bruno Latour says, that the world is inexpressibly complex, and changing all the time – what looks like confusion is a manifestation of this complexity. Transformative as that is on culture and opinion and belief and even on what people are prepared to kill for, it is simply another way of explaining – better or worse, who knows? – the same thing that the old view was trying to explain. The world goes on as it does, and our understanding of it slowly mutates. Which is my subject in this book, boys: the world and everything in it.

There is no indication that the rest of the car is even awake, except for Teeth's earnest concentration on the road ahead and Jackie's gentle sleepy pinching of the skin on the back of my hand. So I end my dissertation with a description of the sculptor Bob and his washer-bending program and I applaud his serious artistic intent. And the proposition that an artist must work on what he must – because life goes on – and let the references, the texture, the critical associations, the explanations, the success, take care of themselves in the grand mutations of the world.

That wakes them up: "That Bob!" They say. "Old Rumpleforeskin!" Hilarity is restored. "If he keeps fiddling with his washers long enough he'll have the pieces to make a car!"

"Like the monkeys with the infinite typing and the random Hamlet!"

"He could call it the Bobmobile!" Howls of laughter.

And then Bald starts telling us all about Teeth's new girlfriend who's a stripper. No she's not, says Teeth. She takes her clothes off and then turns them inside out and puts them back on. That's not stripping, that's art, he says. And all five of us, including little Jackie, who's beginning to get the hang of this, howl with laughter all over again.

WHEN WE ARRIVE IN AACHEN the sky is clear and cold and The Dom is spectacular, sharp as ice in the low winter sunshine. It is a huge dome topped double octagon from 800 AD buried inside the cathedral that has been gradually built around it ever since. The most recent addition being the ticket office, where sits a woman who looks as if she has been waiting for us all day. Her face cracks open with pleasure when we come giggling into the foyer. And then into the dusky ornate space itself, which seems to gather up everything in one sheer move, a sweeping round and up and over all packed together. And this it does every split second of every minute, as it has been doing for a thousand years. It's doing it right now. The place is electrifying. Vertiginous. Jackie grabs my hand and holds tight as we cross the vast floor in and out of flashes of light from the stained glass like spaceships traversing outer space.

But what does it all mean? Charlemagne's bones, or the dust of them, lie in a gold casket covered in images of the Imperium right at the centre. The Dom was built as a copy of the church at Ravenna, the last stronghold of the Western Roman Empire after the barbarian catastrophe, to affirm Charlemagne's claim to the title of Roman emperor. To affirm the unity of his Empire. This is why it has a dome; domes mean *unity*. The walls and the roof are one, my son. It's an essay in everything-speak. The problem is that inside there is unity, one thing, as elaborately portrayed as a forest of trees. But outside, as always, there is everything: the Cathedral is, after all, just one piece of the whole wide world.

"Do you know what this is?" I say to Jackie. "It's a conjuring trick." He looks at me in total ignorance, total agreement. "The builders of this place were trying to make heaven on earth. Not a bad ambition, but a hopeless one." He looks up at me wide-eyed because he knows there's a secret coming; I'm his dad. "Heaven doesn't exist. Earth is as good as it gets."

15

Our Dear Lord in the Attic

The day after the trip to Aachen, Lola has found a spare couple of hours in her busy schedule and we are due to meet at the hidden church just up the canal from our house. She sent a bad-tempered text to arrange it without the usual little string of x's in it. The coincidence of the location in view of what I've seen at Aachen the day before would make my heart leap if it wasn't for the tone of that text. What can I do?

Stay calm. Let the buildings speak. The hidden church is a Catholic chapel called *Ons' Lieve Heer op Zolder*. 'Our Dear Lord in the Attic'. It was built into the top three floors of a big merchant's house in the sixteen sixties because at that time it was illegal for Catholics to practice their faith. A hundred years earlier it was being a protestant that could get you thrown on a bonfire, but by the time this church was secreted into its attic, the shoes were on the other feet, and the Catholic mass had to be held in hiding. Hence the construction of the hidden church. *Hidden* is hardly the word for it now, however – the place is a popular tourist destination curated to the hilt by zealous historians. The whole house has become in their hands an anteroom to the church, in a complete reversal of its seventeenth century function. A reversal that its beauty survives.

Buildings have an inside and an outside. *Dom.* But what this place adds is that in between the inner lining and the outer shell, there is a strangely configured space that is not one or the other. In medium and small sized buildings, there are cellars and stair-cases as well as roof spaces that are too inconveniently shaped to have habitation, and so get used for storage or for games of hide and seek or are commandeered by vermin – and this last is one little mentioned reason why the modern age, in which hygienic science figures strongly, and in which every function has to be accounted for the sake of efficiency, tries to eliminate the difference between outside and inside, and squeeze out undesignated space.

Out on the Polders, the new Dutch lands reclaimed from the sea in the middle of the last century, there is a model village built to house the new modern peasants. The village, Nagele, is arranged round big rectangular greens, full of sun and health, but it is made up of little flat roofed, cubic houses, with tiny rooms. The designers strongly disapproved of the old peasant habit, cravenly hierarchic, of using the kitchen as a family room and keeping a front room for "best", and so made the kitchens as efficient – for which read *small* – as possible. But there, in the village museum, you can see photographs of the inhabitants, families of six or seven, crammed into those little two by two kitchens trying to live life as they knew it. It's hilarious! Today, the village has heritage status and its little houses are occupied by the middle classes, who have a lot more possessions than those peasants ever had. Where to put them? In the attic, maybe? No. There are no pitched roofs and therefore no attics; and the heritage status of the place means no alterations. This is modern life. Everything must be accounted for. There is no slack in it.

In big old buildings, by contrast, the spaces in between the inner lining and the outer shell are big enough to be places in their own right. The configurations of the outside of the inside against the inside of the outside make extraordinary shaped rooms, technically useless and also hidden in the sense of *hardly ever seen*. Beneath the pitched roofs of the old Cathedrals you will find big dark rooms with undulating stone floors made by the tops of the nave arches, and, hanging from the rafters, chains suspending chandeliers into the interior of the church far below that pass through holes in this curving floor, little eyes through which warmth and the echoing sound of prayers and the glitter of candles seep. Astounding atmospherics, all made out of slack.

It is the secret that visitors to the Aachen Dom passing through that ticket office do not see. This house that holds the hidden church in Amsterdam is not cathedral sized, but the top two floors have been partly removed to expand the in-between, and leave a high tiered space full of icons and bleeding figures and the silver rayed monstrance of the Catholic sect. And it is in this elaborate, gilded place that I find Lola standing, frowning, impatiently thumping the audio guide she has hired at the front desk on the back of a chair.

"What have I done?" comes out of my mouth. Get it over with. No time like the present.

"I don't know. Perhaps *Katrina* could tell me," with a blast of frost, "if you introduced us."

Lola doesn't keep stuff inside for long. Down the canal from here is the building in which Anne Frank hid from the Nazis. She too was secreted into a piece of slack space. Lola's own family, Jews like the Franks, was sliced in half by the same terror, but I think if Lola had been Anne Frank she would have given the game away, she would have had to explode and burst out of hiding. The last time a conversation ran up about the brutality of the state of Israel phosphor-bombing Gaza, she reacted: she won't stay quiet. She refers to the astonishing survival of Jewish culture as unequalled in humanity. "The escape from the Pharoes was three and a half thousand years ago – we're still here, where are the Pharoes? The Assyrians and the Babylonians overran us but we're still here – where are they?" She holds that while the Jewish diaspora maintained, as it did in spite of successive persecutions over thousands of years, the Jews were part of the complexity of the world, part of everything. It was that complication that the Nazis tried to simplify by separating Jews out of the mix and concentrating them into camps, in order to carry through their extermination. The Final Solution was intended to make "a better world", says Lola, and look what happens when you try to make the world a better place. That's the irony of the concentration that the state of Israel has become. She says the problem is not just a moral problem, it's also an aesthetic one. Because this imagined better place is always static. It's a picture. It's *picturesque*. The world, she says, is dynamic, alternately warmed and cooled by its proximity to the sun, Spinning through space, tugged this way and that by the moon, the sexual activity of its occupants perpetually recasting the genetic permutations of life; etcetera. *Dynamic*: as is the diaspora.

I love this woman. I call her the *Featherweight Nietzsche* because she knows that every being is its own miracle. She allows her thoughts to be buffeted by nature and history but not by convention. I love Katrina, too, which is difficult to explain – I take a deep breath and try to anyway, try to articulate how she has a lover – lovers – how yes I'm jealous, how my jealousy of them could be Platonic, if there is such a thing as Platonic jealousy, probably not, and find myself floundering, exactly as I should have expected.

"Listen," she says, breaking cover. "You may be able to like everything. But it's a whole other thing to love everybody. When you've worked your way out of the labyrinth, let me know. But have it done by this evening."

AT BLENHEIM PALACE in Oxfordshire there is a secret garden known as Rosamond's bower where Henry the Second kept his mistress Rosamond Clifford. It was accessed through a labyrinth to keep her safe. Or was she a prisoner? The building was locked with a maze instead of a door, to which you had to know the combination as a sequence of left and right turns. The slack I am looking for here is the dead end of the maze. I need to see Katrina.

And as I'm making my way across town on the swerving, clanking tram, I find myself sitting behind a woman with no arms, who is loudly telling the man she is with about her life as an actor. One of her points is how, as an actor, she can play anyone. Hedda Gabler, Beatrice, Barbarella, you name it, she'll do it. The problem is the prejudice of the audiences, who can't see beyond the cripple they see. This prejudice extends, she says in the very next sentence – apparently unable to see the contradiction – to disabled characters being played by able bodied actors: no one would think now of black-facing a white actor to play a black character, so why let an able body play disabled?

"But you just said actors can play anyone!" I want to yell at her.

The baby is delivered from the material constraint of the womb – which has just got too damn small, great as it is – and laid to rest in his cot of contracts. He howls at the discomfort of the release. He gets used to it. Turns fifteen, perceives the crooked structure of the world, howls against it. Gets used to that, too. Grows to manhood. Comes to think of political structures as a workable alternative to freedom. Bribery, nepotism, democracy – whatever works, works. Until it's delivered – then he howls.

I pull out my phone and call Katrina. I tell her about the trouble I'm in. Marital strife!

"Did you tell her about Bamba? She says.

"I couldn't bring myself to say his name." And I didn't add, *she knows about him already*.

"Something's happened. He's gone missing. I've got to find him." And then it begins to snow all over again.

16

Intensive care

The journey back out to IJburg is slow and faltering, like a metaphor for the state I'm in. The tram driver eases his ship along the icy rails with exaggerated care. At one point he stops, gets out holding a crowbar, and checks that the points on the interchange are properly aligned. Then off we slide again towards the bridge and past the huge sluice that controls the level of the inland waterways. The water in the drizzle of the night looks flat and dark and cold and terrible as suicide. I start to think gloomily of the impossibility of how to love everybody. Sex is the drive to separate, not combine, is my drift. Sex mixes genes not to unify, but to split and speciate. It is the drive towards form. The heavy potential of life that females carry in their unfertilized eggs is like an atom bomb, a seriously unstable element that gets knocked out of equilibrium by an explosion. *A sex bomb!* That leaves everyone in the vicinity not flattened, but reconfigured.

When I finally get to Katrina's house, the first thing I see is Bamba's car parked in the street. No one inside. Tyres still warm. So he's there too – which means I'll have to include him in this Lola/Katrina deal, dammit. I deep breathe my way up to the door to lower the anxiety and press the bell. Fronk opens it; "Fuck, not you as well," he says. Inside there is an atmosphere of disarray and tension. Two enormous women are sitting on the tiny plywood kitchen chairs, the flesh of their thighs gently overlapping the seats, holding cans of beer. Fronk opens the fridge door and hands me one. "I suppose you want a glass," he scowls.

What is this? Where's Katrina?

"I'm Serine," one of the women says. "And that's Willow."

Willow says hi, with a little coquettish wave. "We're old friends of Bamba. Do you know Bamba?" I nod at her. The lips in her big face are painted shiny red. I suddenly recall a couple of pigs I saw once standing in a field, female in front, male behind. They were both huge. She stood there still as a statue while he licked her arse noisily, lapping her up like food in a trough. "I guess I should say we're associates, to be exact," she says.

Just then little Jacob bursts into the kitchen and takes a flying leap onto Willow's lap. She is so mountainously slippery that he slides straight off again, and in sliding clutches at her flesh to save himself. Handful over handful, he pulls himself all the way up again. She laughs and ruffles his hair and gives him a cavernous hug and holds him there while he wriggles. "We got to sit here, we got to wait." She says to him.

Fronk leaves the room and we can hear him stamping up the stairs. Then stamping down again. He beckons at me from the door

"They've been here all day!" he hisses. "It's driving Jacob mad. Did you see the way she was touching him?"

She was giving him a hug!" I say. There is a twitch of the puritan about Fronk. I can imagine him in a previous life pointing out witches to the authorities. "Who are they?"

"Two of Bamba's donkeys," he says. "They've been here all day. It's driving Jacob mad," he says again. "Katrina's not here. She's gone to the cuckoo's nest with Bamba."

"What happened?"

"I told you. We're getting ready to go there now."

"Can I bring Lola?"

Before he can say *what do I care?* Serine barges out of the kitchen jangling the car keys. "Come on, we'll go get Lola," she says to me.

"Who's Lola?" calls out Willow.

"See you at the Cuckoo's Nest," Serine says to Fronk. He grunts. "See you later, little man," she says to Jacob, and Fronk grabs him and hoists him off the ground to safety.

SERINE AND I GO FLYING DOWN THE HIGHWAY in sumptuous style, soft brown leather, polished walnut and satin chrome strips like an ocean liner, and a galaxy of little red lights making our faces glow in the dark. Serine's wedged into the driving seat, voluptuously gripped by the seatbelt. Her bulk makes her look like a truck driver, but she handles the wheel with grace and her long pink nails are wrapped round a cigarette, which she draws at strongly with those fat red lips.

She pulls a long loop south to come up to the centre city via the road alongside the Amstel River, and her route takes us past the big hospital. I can see the grey masses of it three blocks away behind the trees lining the road. The hospital is, like the airport, a small city in itself; a collection of grey clad blocks with green glass looking like the future past. Punctuated by tall chimneys puffing invisible gases into the sky, and set in a wide landscape of kerbs and grass and asphalt marked up like the deck of a warship.

Not so long ago Jackie pitched up there in intensive care after a nasty episode which had us fearing for his life. He went the colour of a boiled beetroot and his heart rate pushed up to a hundred and ninety and we thought it was going to burst. He survived – but I remember going back there on the second day with a strong sense of disaster. I could feel the wind from death's hammer slamming against the anvil. The Intensive Care Unit is a long distance from the main entrance. I had to go through a succession of automatic glass doors, down corridors, past department after department and their festivals of signage, and finally up an elevator with a tragic-comic collection of casualties in it. A care worn man in pyjamas pushing his drip stand and clutching a pack of cigarettes, wearing his name and number on a little plastic bracelet like an inmate. A whole family, aunts, uncles, parents, children, all carrying flowers. A mother holding the hand of a vacant eyed child with a shaved head. The stress was palpable. The taking it one day at a time existing right there in the suffering present was slathered all over everyone. Me too: I felt for us all, as I clutched Jackie's box of chocolates in my hand.

When the door dinged open at floor seventeen and I emerged into the Intensive Care Unit reception I was confronted by a posse of policemen guarding the door. And one police woman, who was passing chocolates round to her mates. They looked at me suspiciously, and froze like statues. They had blue uniforms with straps, and black Berettas holstered in their belts. One of them searched me before I went in, pulling on a pair of bright blue rubber gloves to pat me all over. Is this usual?

Through the big doors, built to last with their toughened glass and their kick plates and their expensive ironmongery, and into a big, dimly lit ward full of curtains and medical machinery and empty beds. I passed the nursing station where five people dressed in pale blue smocks were sitting and talking quietly and eating chocolates. The place was awash with chocolates.

Straight ahead was a body covered in bandages and covered in folds of cloth connected up to a phalanx of life support robots, whose monitors clicked and blinked with each slow breath. He lay flat on his back with his eyes closed, looking like a Pharaoh in some ancient tomb. He was one of only two patients in there; and to the left, sitting up in a pool of light with his mother, was the other one. Trogo, smiling all over his face.

"Hey, lucky man," I said. "The man who prays on the ocean is himself an ocean of peace." He reached out and pulled me over close to him and the relief washed over me like a breaking wave.

Intensive care. It's what the world needs. If we took intensive care of everything like these people do their patients, cliff face earth would be okay. But it's not the interventions that make intensive care, not the armory of medication that is so impressive, it's the intense observation. That's what we should be doing to the world. Like a painter looks at it; closely observing. Every ten minutes a nurse came by and checked the numbers on Jackie's machinery and the flow on his drip.

One of the nurses stayed longer than the others, and leant over the bed to lay healing hands upon him. She looked up at me. She and Lola exchanged smiles. "Is this him?" She said.

"This is him."

I looked at Lola. "Okay, what are the police all for?" I said. They both laughed.

"I see what you mean!" Said the nurse. And then Lola:

"shhh! Idiot! The police are guarding that one over there!" pointing to the body lying on the catafalque on the other side of the room.

"That's gangster number two. He's going to give evidence against gangster number one," said the nurse.

"If he survives," said Lola.

Serine sits silently piloting the big car through the tiny streets while I'm remembering all this. She looks over and asks me what I'm smiling about. And I tell her I was thinking about the cuckoo's nest. I've only just got the joke. On the way out of the intensive care when I passed the nursing station, one lonely chocolate was sitting in its foil in the box, like the last egg in the nest. The survivor. "Take it," They said. "No one likes to take the last one in here. It's unlucky." I stuck it in my mouth and sneaked a quick look at gangster number two. Still breathing. Next, click, next, click, next, went the monitor; life in the Intensive Care ward is so finely balanced it's measured in breaths, in by out by in by out – like transcendental meditation. Except that in there, becoming one with the universe is what they're trying to stop.

17

The Cuckoo's Nest

Lola is standing by the window looking at a big book when I come into the room, with the Old Church in the background behind a layer of lace, and the low winter sun illuminating her from behind. There's a line of gold light tracing the outline of her head and the heavy folds of the dress she's wearing is falling off into shadows. It's like looking at a painting by Vermeer – as soft and delicate as that. Her refracted mood of earlier on has gone, but when she sees me she pulls the heavy book towards her body as if she's closing a door. Then she recants and holds it out, open, and shows me an old Dutch painting of the Madonna and child, painted in fourteen eighty something. No one knows exactly when. It's called *The Holy Kinship*. The two of them are surrounded by the child's aunts and cousins, and are all sitting in a richly decorated church with wide open walls that show the landscape beyond, with trees and other buildings; men of various stations in life, baskets of fruit, flowers, tasselled bows. There is a tiled floor that looks like a map. And on the altar of the church there is a statue of an execution, with the victim blindfolded and kneeling and the executioner swinging a heavy scimitar. The detail is astounding. What a find. It looks like the painter was trying to paint everything.

I tell her that I want her to come and meet Katrina. She is not so sure. But when I tell her we are going to the Cuckoo's Nest and will also meet the great Bamba, Sufi and helper of women, and that we're going in his car with one of those women, then she says okay. And soon there we all are, Jackie and I lolling in the back like two gangsters and Lola and Serine getting on like sisters in the front, our molls.

The cuckoo's nest is a shack out on the polder that Katrina and

Fronk use for summer weekends. The name is a joke because the cuckoo doesn't have a nest of its own, but uses the nests of other birds. It loiters nearby until the nest is full of eggs and then, *opportunistic* evolved-in as surely as the colour of its feathers, darts in and lays one egg in the nest, in fifteen seconds flat, and then flies off to Africa to recover. It is not the most extraordinary story in nature's collection but it is such un-familial behaviour that it alone makes the Earth seem like a distant planet full of aliens. At least that's how it seems on this strange night.

In order to fool the foster birds, cuckoos specialize in laying eggs similar to only one species of bird. The eggs of the cuckoos that lay in warbler's nests look different to the eggs of the cuckoos that lay in wagtail's nests. It is suggested that this is a sort of infantile behaviour, in which the host species is imprinted on the female cuckoo, like an adolescent human mother turning her baby over to its grandmother – is that an actual world soap opera? Also, she doesn't fly off to Africa immediately, but hangs around to see the egg hatch out. If the hosts rumble her and cast out her egg, she might destroy the nest – which sounds like another soap episode, and maybe a reminder that the actual world is the same for the cuckoo as it is for you and me – because the universality of 'everything' means that your actual is the same for everything – and that it is not in the actual world but in the real that these cuckoo egg dramas take place. The birds and bees have their real worlds too.

THE CABIN IS WAY OUT OF TOWN on the edge of a moonlit mere fringed with reeds. We slip off the highway onto a country road that runs alongside a forest below the dike and goes as straight as forever until the headlights show a gated junction, where we turn into the trees. Serine works the big black car down a track lined both sides with thorn bushes until we break out into a small clearing and there is the cabin, just a wooden hut, standing darkly in the centre. Serine stops the car and turns the key and the engine dies and she breathes out into the stillness as though she's been holding her breath all the way.

"There it is," she says. "The Cuckoo's Nest."

"Where is everybody?"

"They'll be here. Relax," she says. And on cue, enter from the left Katrina and Bamba, laughing, carrying bundles of firewood like a pair of peasants. Darkness, stillness, laughter, the dancing flames of a wood fire: anxiety could not survive this environment. Katrina and Lola came together immediately in warm diplomacy. I was expecting frost and I got thaw.

"Hey, lucky man," said Bamba. "The man who prays on the ocean is himself an ocean of peace." He goes over to Lola and takes her hand and the charm flows like he's thrown a switch. He leads her into the cabin whispering things I can't hear and Katrina slides up close to me and starts to slowly rub my back.

We are on the edge of a shallow lake called the *Oostvaardersplassen*. It means 'Fishermen's Lake'. When the polders were drained fifty years ago this piece was left as it was, in a very early piece of nature conservation. The polders are strange pieces of land to think about because they are human made – as flat as the seabed they once were, surrounded by dikes and lying below sea level – and you can feel the strangeness just standing in them. *Unnatural* would be one word for it. The process was to build a ring dike around an area of maybe seven hundred square kilometres, then pump out all the seawater – a task that on its own takes ten years – then seed the salty ground with reeds using aeroplanes, then another ten year wait while the reeds leech the salt out of the soil, then plough the whole thing back into the ground and at last start planting crops. The strangeness of the process is masked by the cheerful colonization by the biomass in all its forms that turns these sheets of engineered graph paper into ordinary nature – but still, the mind is taxed, what is this new land? And to put it in the terms of this book, is it everything or nothing?

The *Oostvaardersplassen* is one answer. The area was set aside from the reclamation project as a nature reserve behind a high fence and then left as it was to evolve. Literally left untouched. Humans are not allowed in there, not even wardens. Anything could be happening behind the fence. It is a human made wilderness, which adds another dimension of strangeness to an already strange place: it intimates how doubly unnatural the idea of conservation is.

The six of us sit by Katrina's new fire and I tell them my favourite conservation folly story, the story of the Ruddy Duck. It's a story about hating change, and the violence that springs from that. A story about the force of stasis. It is not an ugly duckling story, but a beautiful duck story. The Ruddy Ducks, *Oxyura jamaicensis,* have russet feathers and beaks as blue as the sky and their tails are pointed like spears. The males are famously horny in the world of ducks and in courtship display they stick their tails straight up in the air and hammer the water with their beaks so that it foams up over their chests and seems to make them look twice as big. They are duck studs. So much so that even the females of other species will mate with them!

A clutch of these ducks were imported into an ornamental duck pond in England, but escaped and went feral, and now, maybe because of their fecundity, they are thriving wild. But that is not the end of it. The Ruddy Ducks are not a native species, say the conservationists from the Royal Society for the Protection of Birds. Their very horniness suggests that they will interbreed with – and eclipse – the native stiff tail species, which are already on the danger of extinction list. *They are over sexed and over here! They must be exterminated!* And this is why, every winter, they go out with guns to try and shoot every Ruddy Duck in the country dead. What kind of protection racket is that?

The lights of a car arriving outside wash the inside of the cabin and Fronk and Jacob and Willow come through the door bringing boxes of food and wine and the party gets going. Jacob and Jackie sit together on the floor playing a wordless game, Serine and Willow and Lola and Katrina sit in a circle like the women in that *Holy Kinship* painting and Bamba and Fronk and I stand in the background chewing the fat like the three wise men. Outside the moon glimmers over a landscape humming with emergence. Is this a happy ending? Or is there no such a thing as an ending if we live in the present?

The cuckoo chick hatches out before the other eggs and the fledgling sets about heaving them out of the nest until it is the only one left. Then, while its hoodwinked parent-carers – and *parent-carer*, by the way, is what they call you if you're the father of a disabled child – fill their every minute with foraging for food and stuffing it into its ever open mouth, it grows and grows and grows and grows. Until there is the comical and violent sight of the tiny bird feeding a chick three times as big as itself.

"Look at the size of my chick, man," screeches the little bird proudly. "Isn't he the best thing you ever saw?!"

What do you do with the tyranny of the present? Fill it with action: feed that thing! Pursue truth, find beauty, do goodness. Thank you, little bird.

"BAMBA'S SO HANDSOME," Lola says on the way home. Oh yes? "But he's crazy!" What did he say to her? "About how Sufis train themselves to watch the world coming into being. That's how they pray." What's crazy about that? The Sufi understands his place in the present instant. The creation for him is the continuous emergence of everything. "He said they live so completely in the present that they have no hope of heaven or fear of hell. And he had a message for you, too."

"What kind of a message?"

"Your kind of message," she says. "He said your 'Everything' is a replacement for 'Unity'. There's no *absolute truth*, but there is *absolutely everything*."

He knows where I live. The speculative philosophers drive

towards a dissolute present to keep possibilities open while the forces of stasis attempt to shut them down – but look at us. Living fragments. Committed and emergent at the very same time. And time is the duration of your *commitment*, otherwise known as your *life*.

Do you remember the problem of the duration of the present? The present is so short, it carries no information, and therefore it's unperceivable. The instant of the present is invisible. But this message from Bamba is that the *duration of your life* is only one solution. In that moment of the present, there is absolutely everything, because of the *only possible world* – otherwise known as the *actual world* – and this could be the location of the truth. We can't see it, because the instant of the present has no information. So we see the world refracted through the lens of our real world, which is nothing but information. Pigeons, crows, seagulls, cuckoos – they all have their real worlds too. They can't see the actual either. But there it is.

"He's a crank," she says, my featherweight Nietzsche. My glamorous spy. But *I* think the only cranky part is that the Sufis think it's all caused by a supreme being, and not by the rotations of the universe. By *Spacetime*. "Oh yes, Atheist," she says. "And you know what? That sounds cranky too!"

The Bowl of the Horizon

I once worked on a regeneration program in Hackney, London, a poor part of town since the beginning. Somewhere the planners and financiers of the regeneration were hacking their way through meetings with fat cats, but I, artist, writer, found myself at the soft end of the program talking to local ten year olds about the material world. Children are so accepting of the world they find themselves in that the word 'regeneration' – making the world anew – is meaningless. This lot didn't yet know how poor they were, how prejudice worked, how much luck played a part in fulfilling ambition – they were ten, and their futures were full of themselves. I wanna be a pop star, said Rhianna, I wanna be a glamour girl, said Carly, I wanna play football for Arsenal, said Emil, and I'm gonna be a millionaire and have a big dog and a big television and a big house. They were ten. It was only a matter of three or four years before society took its carefully nurtured discriminations and inequalities and unfairness and flung it all straight in their faces. But I was hoping that we could at least trap some coherent thoughts or attitudes that would skew the regeneration in their favour.

So I got them drawing maps of the things they encountered on the way to school, to expose what sort of a material world mattered to them. I wasn't going for a subjective analysis like a Situationist, but rather looking for a measure of it all, of the ambient accumulation of material. What's ambient? They said. I explained that one day soon we will be recharging our phones with energy harvested from the waves of radio transmission ambient in the air around us. Do we breath radio waves, then? Well, no. But we'll charge our phones from the energy they transmit themselves? Well, yes. Now start drawing!

The first boy I spoke to showed me his map and pointed out the huge dog turd by the post box, covered in green flies which fled at the mere hint of your shadow, and the McDonalds' carton with the half eaten hamburger in it by the pedestrian crossing. Mundane stuff – but he turned out to be an artist in the making. "Have you noticed," he said, "that everywhere you look, the rooftops are joined to the sky?" It was the poor part of town, and the day was full of poignancy – this horizon specialist had never been to the seaside to see that fabulous blue on blue of the sky and the sea. But what he said fledged the thought that all round our heads, as far as our eyes can see, is the edge of the actual world. Never mind the distant truth: we live in our observations. We live in the bowls of ourselves, whose rims are at the height of our eyes above the ground, and everything inside the bowl is us as much as it is the world. I thought that this boy was a twenty-first century boy: that he carried the future without knowing it. But then I moved on to Carly with her black patent shoes and her eyes smeared with the remnants of the makeup she was not allowed to wear inside the school gates. "Look," she said, showing me her map. "There's the dog-mess by the post box and here's that McDonalds carton with the rotten burger in it."

We live in the bowls of ourselves, whose rims are at the height of our eyes above the ground, and everything inside your bowl is you as much as it is the world. The swooping parallaxes and the continual shifts in perspective you go through every day are like the bowl's mental optics. Your pack of perceptions. They shift with your relative height, your relative solitude and your relative mood. The quantum physicists used to say that the observer's presence changes the event observed. What if that event is itself the observer – is it that that makes the truth a personal matter?

The next session with the children was a visit to Greenwich Park, which has a big hill at its centre with a statue of General Wolfe on it. Appropriate – it was he who scaled the heights of Quebec in the English and French colonial wars. Hackney is as flat as the river flood plain it is, so this meeting with the hill was profound. They were poor, remember, and ten years old. They didn't travel much and they had never visited this place, only ten kilometres from their own homes. You could see the whole of the city and the hills beyond from the top of that hill. I arranged them all in a circle on the grass and we tried an experiment. Hold still, I said, as still as you can. And look hard at the horizon. Feel the weight of your head and hold it as steady as you can. Feel every swallow and every blink. This bowl of the world whose rim is the horizon is the wilderness you inhabit. It could be that you have *fallen there, body heart and mind together; it could be that you have chosen to be there. Whichever way, it is your world. Your head and those others all around you are linked not as a community, but as islands in an ocean of possibilities, each head a lighthouse beaming out the presence of the edge of another piece of wilderness. Together, you are witnesses to the world.*

Back in the classroom, a girl from Sierra Leone said her family were refugees from the war, because the war meant there was nothing to eat. She was different from the others – she had travelled maybe too much. The floor of her bowl was strewn with strife. What will happen if god takes everything away? She said. Because of all the wars we fight, if he takes everything away we won't have anything to eat. We could always eat each other, I said. That's stupid what you say, she replied, we can't eat each other. Then she showed me her map. It was full of butterflies and plants.

What mattered to them? Everything. They each lived in a world with everything in it, everything mattered and they liked it all.

6
Everything Again

The conclusions that we seek to draw from the likeness of events are unreliable, because events are always unlike.

Montaigne, *On Experience*

18

Everything

When I came to Amsterdam to write this book, I thought criticism and creativity were clean different things. I thought that one was about use and the other about making, and that the theories of use – critical theories – had grown like thorn thickets around the arts of making and enmired them in critical protocols: *the tail is wagging the dog!* as the old guys used to say. I thought that art had been diverted from its purpose of exploring perception and that artists had become so bogged down by critical practice they could no longer act – that they could no longer tell their means from their ends. I thought that discrimination and dialectic had become a curse and that deliberately setting out to like everything would be a way to counter that. How To Like Everything is a utopia, I thought, a utopia that could be made simply by reframing our stance to the world around us.

Now, having been dragged through the briars by Bamba and Katrina and Lola and Fronk and Bob and the anaconda and the Inquisition, not to mention Jackie, whose congenital inability to conform has floodlit my desire to pitch what's emergent against what's usual, I need to reframe the distinction between criticism and creativity. I said before that evolution and creation are not opposites, but two attempts to explain the same phenomenon; so, criticism and creativity are both wrapped up together in the questions of how we use the world and how we abstract it. It is not that art must be liberated from criticism – but that criticism could be liberated from itself. It could act from inside its subjects, spurring their trajectories, wobbling their orbits and sharing in their evolutionary opportunism. Let the dog start wagging the tail again. And think again of Beauty, Truth and Goodness: they could be approached not as ideals, but as actions and passions intertwined. As means *and* ends. We *find* beauty, we *pursue* truth and we *do* goodness.

It is not only artists who engage with the actual world through abstraction. The entire human artifice – everything we make and do – is a huge collection of abstractions. This shade of utility is speciesist rather than humanist: It doesn't elevate human consciousness above all else; it is merely partisan for humanity. We abstract the world differently to crows because we are different from crows. But we are powerful. Our abstractions inflect the world more than theirs. I once stood in the park – an abstraction of wilderness – and watched a squirrel rooting through a waste bin, picking out possible things to eat and flinging the leftovers on the ground. A pair of crows stood by the bin picking over what it threw away, looking up at it for what came next like black-feathered beggars. It was funny to see. It looked like the squirrel was feeding the birds.

AND NOW WE'RE ON A DAY TRIP to Rotterdam. We have sunshine, warm breezes and clemency. The weather has changed, like a benign catastrophe. It feels like the first day of spring already and it's still January. Lola and Jackie and I are in the beautiful old Boijmans Museum, standing in front of *The Holy Kinship*, the painting Lola was looking at yesterday in that big book.

Before coming here we took the tourist cruise ship that runs down to the working part of the river. Rotterdam is a huge port and full of the world's trade. A long and intricate system of docks plays host to ship after ship after ship after ship. Filthy as hard work, streaked with rust and spume and seagull shit, with strange alphabets on their sides from all over the world, coded Chinese, Korean, Russian. Great stacks of blue and brown and red containers stand at the docksides casting shadows deep as mountains. Cranes throng the sky. And through all this heavy commerce, for a long hour, our pristine white cruiser slipped like a snooper. The three of us stood up on the top deck open to a balmy sky that seemed as big as the planet itself exalting in the glory of the wide world. While downstairs, in the lounge, a party of young teens barely older than Jackie but heavily neuro-typical, sat round tables smoking and playing poker and not looking out of the windows at all.

Rotterdam is a twentieth century city, bombed flat by all sides in the last great European war and rebuilt from the rubble up. New docks, new houses, new shops, offices and factories. New parks. It still quivers with the toil of the rebuilding like a chisel-hewn jungle. It's so uncompromising that the people who live there have taken on progress as one of life's great jokes. Try as hard as they can to love their city, they can't. They build buildings that slope and posture like comedians, and they say that the Amsterdammers are *fairies* who live in *dolls houses*. But: in the middle of this windy, assertive place-of-now stands the Boijmans museum, a 1930's flapper of a building, silken-fringed, flat-chested, sublime, that somehow escaped the swarm of bombs. It has thin brown bricks and fancy green copper roofs and intricate stone dressings. It is a museum of art. The contemporary collection is a mixed bag of gestures and pouts like the city itself, but then upstairs there are the old masters. Room after room of painstakingly detailed Dutch paintings painted with tiny brushes apparently made from eyelashes that show miracles happening in ordinary life, like *The Holy Kinship* we've come to see.

The Holy Kinship is a late medieval idea that set out to show Christ as a king by stressing his dynastic attributes. So in the painting he, the baby, looking as wise as Jesus already, sits on Mary's lap next to Mary's mother Anne and her cousin Elizabeth and Elizabeth's baby son who will grow up to be John the Baptist. His father and uncle and the original patriarch Jesse are at the door and his future disciples, boys of Jackie's age, are sitting on the floor breaking open a barrel of beer. In their elaborate setting they look like a pack of animals living in a gilded jungle. The pack is a baby's introduction to life outside its own little ecology of the womb. It is the first horizon. Kid's stuff. That's what makes this a picture of everything.

Later, in the cafe, I contemplate my own little intense threesome. St. Trogo, St. Paul and the immaculate Lola, surrounded by the artifacts of contemporary life. Who will paint us, and why? There is the actual world, flashing past us at incomprehensible speed: there stand the artists trying to see it. Everyone catches a different glimpse, everyone tries to show what they see of it to everyone else; and these abstractions of the actual, these splinters of perception, are the content of art. Looked at like this, even the most realistic representations are abstractions; even photographs are abstractions. Every art is abstract art. Artists stand there before the ongoing emergence of the world making their approximations as best they can. And why? Because someone has to do it.

On the way out we pass the rooms where the Boijmans museum keeps its minimalist sculpture. Minimal means, among other things, no names. So: shining steel cubes on the floor, blank canvases and rows of coloured fluorescent light tubes pinned to the wall like trophies. The works are famous for not being abstractions, but for being real. As the placard on the wall says, "These works are not *representations* of the real, they *are* the real." But if all art is abstraction, how can that be? Does the distinction between *real* and *actual* worlds clarify it? Are these mute minimalist lumps in the end like those bourgeois paintings of second empire high couture, pictures of fashionable women perfectly dressed, immaculate pieces of the real world imagined by humans?

The next room has only one piece in it, a large steel cage painted German Army grey. In fact it is a double cage, a cage within a cage, within the room. The outer cage is an impressively logical arrangement of components incorporating doors that would allow, were this not a museum, access to the narrow separation between the outer and inner cages. The inner cage holds nothing. The affirmatively separated out space between the inner and outer cages flows easily through all its parts, but it also is empty. Jackie goes right ahead anyway and squeezes in there, and grins at us like an animal in the zoo.

It was WH Auden who said that 'poetry makes nothing happen'. For Auden, nothing being something was a modernist game. But an *abstraction* of nothing like this cage is a pretty hefty game to play. It seems to stop time. And I think of the actual gorilla in his cage in the zoo, waiting for nothing to happen. Living in the present, day after day, year after year, until he dies. My god! Is that art, too?

ALL THE WAY BACK TO AMSTERDAM on the train, Jackie is having a hard time. He lives like that gorilla. Imprisoned by the present or liberated by it we do not know. *What's going to happen next?* He asks again and again. *How will we know when we get there?* Where the average citizen carries an understanding of the workings of the tram numbers and routes and how the constellations of lines and stops stack up into a picture of the city, to Jackie it might as well be magic. It has been a lesson to me to try and explain how we know the number 16 will go down the Damrak just like it did yesterday; because what is at the bottom of the explanation is that the tram driver has agreed in advance to do it. In fact when you dissect the workings of society, the whole thing depends on contracts and trust, from the money in your pocket to the vows of marriage. It's what the pecking order has become – all backed up by the force of the law as sure as a swipe of the Alpha Male Baboon's claws. It's another description of the real world. In some ways Jackie is more in tune with the present than any of us. Less contaminated by real world abstractions. But how do you know whom you can trust? This train could be going to Siberia and we will be deposited in a land of snow and white tigers and be stuck forever in gulag land.

Every day I thank him for the insights his condition forces out of me. Because now I fall to thinking that this train ride is not just a contract – it is an abstraction of the journey itself, a translation of desire into life. I try to communicate this fledgling thought to Lola, wondering if there could be some sort of brain yoga that Trog could do along the lines of, what shall we call it – *abstraction translation*? But she tops it with a better idea. A technique called Attention Deconcentration.

She says she learnt it from some free divers in Bermuda. These are the guys – and dolls – who go down to 100 metre depths with no oxygen tanks. Obviously being able to hold your breath is the first qualification. They can do it for seven or eight minutes, in a complicated physiological practice that compresses their lungs to the size of a tennis ball. The second qualification is obviously a reckless disregard for personal safety, I am thinking, but far from it. What they are doing in these dives is approaching the boundaries of self-control, all the way to the edge of the abyss of panic. To achieve it they practice a mental calming technique called attention – attention what?

"*Attention de-concentration.*" She says. "What they're looking for is a way of taking in the whole field of perception. Usually when you're working on something you have to concentrate your attention on certain specific tasks, but this is the opposite."

"Why do they do it?"

"It's like meditation, but without the aim to detach. High stress can induce it. Soldiers in action know what it's about. As a *psychotechnic*," as a what? "As a brain control technique – it was invented for people doing intricate and stressful tasks. Like those astronauts who do zero gravity space walks to fix satellites." I've seen the pictures. Hanging in space clutching a socket wrench, tethered by a gold plated umbilical cord, surrounded by infinity. "The divers say that what happens in the deconcentrated state is that anxiety evaporates, and you feel your position among things, and everything becomes part of you. Your consciousness empties out, but you are so in touch with the situation that you can react immediately and without thinking." Are you thinking what I'm thinking? Is this, finally, how to like everything? Maybe call it *Discrimination Deconcentration*?

What you're trying to do with attention deconcentration is to distribute your attention across the whole field. People learning to deconcentrate start by looking straight ahead and observing the periphery of their vision, above, below, left and right, all at the same time. This helps to suspend spontaneous eye movements and focuses attention not on objects, but on fragments of the vision field. If you get it right, your eyes won't cling to objects, or even move. It's hard to learn, because the instinctive way to see is to concentrate on the centre. But when you've mastered it, you expand the practice until it covers not just vision, but all sensations. I look over at Jackie staring out of the window at the hedgerows zipping past. If only he could do this. If only he could learn to take in everything simultaneously and evaporate his anxiety. Then I catch myself; 'if only' is meaningless. *The world could be different, but it's not.*

"How did you meet these diver guys?" I ask her.

"Don't be silly," she says with a smile. "You know I can't tell you that."

THE WINTER'S HALF OVER, and soon we will be leaving Holland. But a nursing home issue has suddenly spun up and I have to make a trip to London to see the solicitor. He has an office nineteen floors up a twenty-storey office building in the city. He has that lawyer's charisma that comes from maintaining positions of certainty for long periods. He likes to make small talk on the way back to the elevator after meetings. He asks what I'm doing in Amsterdam, and when I tell him I'm writing a book called *How To Like Everything*, he says "But liking everything must be nearly impossible." *Nearly.* "Like seeing everything, don't you think? You can see nearly everything, but you can't see your own face," he says, with a look of bemused concern. I try the rest of the slogan on him. Believe in nothing, know what you know, live in the present.

"But if you believe in nothing, how can you explain anything?" he says. "An explanation is a description mapped on to a system of belief. That's basic information theory. It's how the law works. And it's how the world works." The law! I sigh. A house of cards! I say that believing in nothing allows for provisional explanations – it's the way you take on other worlds: a way to explain such things as Shakespeare's racism and Neo Classical architecture's imperialism without derailing your affection for the works themselves. But he has little patience for speculations like that. And I'm grateful to him – his trust in his pack of cards is one of the things that gave me the idea for this *How To Like Everything* project. Along with Jackie's predicament, the story of Little Red Cape and Fronk's image of the Globeskin. The question is how to be free in the real world while knowing that you can't be free in the actual. The law is a systematic discrimination and so is contemporary philosophy. I wanted to try and write without system. I wanted to write *indiscriminately*. At the time I imagined writing a book like one of those plastic postcards covered in tiny grooves, with one image printed on one side of the groove, another on the other. So that every time you shift it slightly the picture changes. That's what I thought this book could be like.

He leaves me pushing the call button on the elevator and strides off back to his office, and I decide to use the stairs instead. When I get out in the stairwell I see the stairs going up as well as down and I find myself climbing instead of descending, and at the top there is a door – unlocked! – that opens onto the roof. I go through it and the actual world suddenly explodes in my face. The enormous sky and a wide-open vista of the city of London, spread out over the landscape as far as I can see, like a thick, elaborate layer of complications pasted over the ground.

Breathtaking. Beautiful. And in that first ecstatic moment with everything suddenly there and the bowl of my horizon suddenly pushed out to a fifty kilometre diameter, I switch straight into the deconcentrated state that Lola's divers were using. It sounded difficult when she described it but up here it happened just like that. It's what city observation towers are for. It's what the tower of Babel was for: to see everything at once. Recall it now – the first time you glimpsed an enormous view, and you suddenly felt elated, pitched out of time, and saw that you were standing on the surface of the planet. On top of the world!

And then, over the next few minutes, your mind takes repossession, and starts to sort and reorganize and construct coherence, and so gradually subdues the ecstasy. I once heard a description by the landscape painter Rackstraw Downes of the effects of closely observing the landscape. He makes intensely realistic – *actualistic* – fresh air paintings of New Jersey, along the Hudson River's convoluted edge, a wasteland of heavy industry and garbage disposal with huge cloudscapes and white-feathered egrets picking their way through the polluted marsh grasses. He loves the minute-by-minute dynamics of light and movement and tries to catch it all. He seems to have trained himself to sustain that first ecstatic moment for the whole two or three months it takes to paint a picture, and with close observation, driven by the desire to get it down exactly right, he says he gradually becomes a part of the scene himself. He's an artist, not a solicitor: he maintains a position of *uncertainty* for long periods. An enquiry is a position of uncertainty. He enters into the web of relationships in the scene, he says, and the man doing the painting becomes as much part of it as the weeds growing in the gutter, or the shifting patterns of traffic on the bridge.

Cranky.

Everything Places are not paradises; they are utopias of the possible. They are vantage points from which you can make out the multiple currents of the world and sense the complexity all gathered up into one fist. On my wall at home I have a picture of Lossiemouth air force base, in Scotland. The olive drab extent of it stretches out across the middle distance. There are the runway strips, the water towers, the control towers, the nuclear blast hardened shelters as big as warehouses and the little grey fighters being readied for the apocalypse. In front of all this is a pig farm, with maybe a hundred galvanized iron pigsties sitting on the pig rooted earth and separated by electric fences, the pink fatness of the animals scattered across the terrain like so many naked four legged humans. My brothers. Behind it is the stone garrison town of Lossiemouth built by the English invaders two hundred years ago, occupying a slight hill on the horizon with the church spire sticking out of the middle, small as a needle at this distance. And behind that is the greater horizon of the ocean and the sky and the mournful mountains, and the forests where the wild deer live.

That's an everything place. So is the vision painted by the master of *The Holy Kinship* in the museum in Rotterdam. So is the top of the city tower. So is the pond in our garden in London with its tiny community of species tangled together in the evolutionary struggle in their two metre cubed world of water. And you know what? The harder you look for everything, the more of it you can find.

I ARRIVE BACK IN AMSTERDAM AT MIDNIGHT and fight my way through the sex-crazed crowds to my dark house and my sleeping family. But when I pass Jackie's room he is sitting up, wide awake. The electric fan he keeps running all night to smooth out the sounds is churning away like a robot waterfall. "Time to get up," he says when he sees me. I wrap him in a blanket and take him by the hand and open the hatch to the roof and we clamber out into the night sky together and survey the bright lights of the city burning like fury. I describe to him the satellite photos of the night-time earth that show pinpoints of lights, the places of human habitation, lit up like stars. We are standing in the middle of the Northern European Galaxy: for in these images the great conurbations of the industrialized world where the pinpoints coalesce are like galaxies. The black oceans and deserts of the Earth are like interstellar space.

I tell Jackie to imagine millions of packs of humans huddled round their campfires in the middle of the dark wilderness. We both look up into the vacant sky trying to see the truth of the universe and we see nothing. We climb into a spaceship and accelerate out into near earth orbit and look back, and see the surface of the earth, and everything on it, a universe in itself.

Acknowledgements

Thanks to Aart Oxenaar, Marijke Hogenboom, Martijn de Wit, Pieter Jannick and Jan Peter Wingender at the Acadamie Van Bouwkunst, Amsterdam

Thanks to Claudia Zeiske at Deveron Arts, Huntly, Aberdeenshire

Thanks to Jem Finer, Andre Dekker, Kathryn Moore, Colette Barrere, Anatoly Travin, Fred Scott, Richard Divers and Liz Flanagan

Parts of this book have been previously published in MAS Context issue 11 and in *Kuntswerken voor de publieke ruimte*, Podium Voor Architectuur Haarlemmermeer en Schiphol

Contemporary culture has eliminated both the concept of the public and the figure of the intellectual. Former public spaces – both physical and cultural – are now either derelict or colonized by advertising. A cretinous anti-intellectualism presides, cheered by expensively educated hacks in the pay of multinational corporations who reassure their bored readers that there is no need to rouse themselves from their interpassive stupor. The informal censorship internalized and propagated by the cultural workers of late capitalism generates a banal conformity that the propaganda chiefs of Stalinism could only ever have dreamt of imposing. Zer0 Books knows that another kind of discourse – intellectual without being academic, popular without being populist – is not only possible: it is already flourishing, in the regions beyond the striplit malls of so-called mass media and the neurotically bureaucratic halls of the academy. Zer0 is committed to the idea of publishing as a making public of the intellectual. It is convinced that in the unthinking, blandly consensual culture in which we live, critical and engaged theoretical reflection is more important than ever before.